Cranach
A–Z

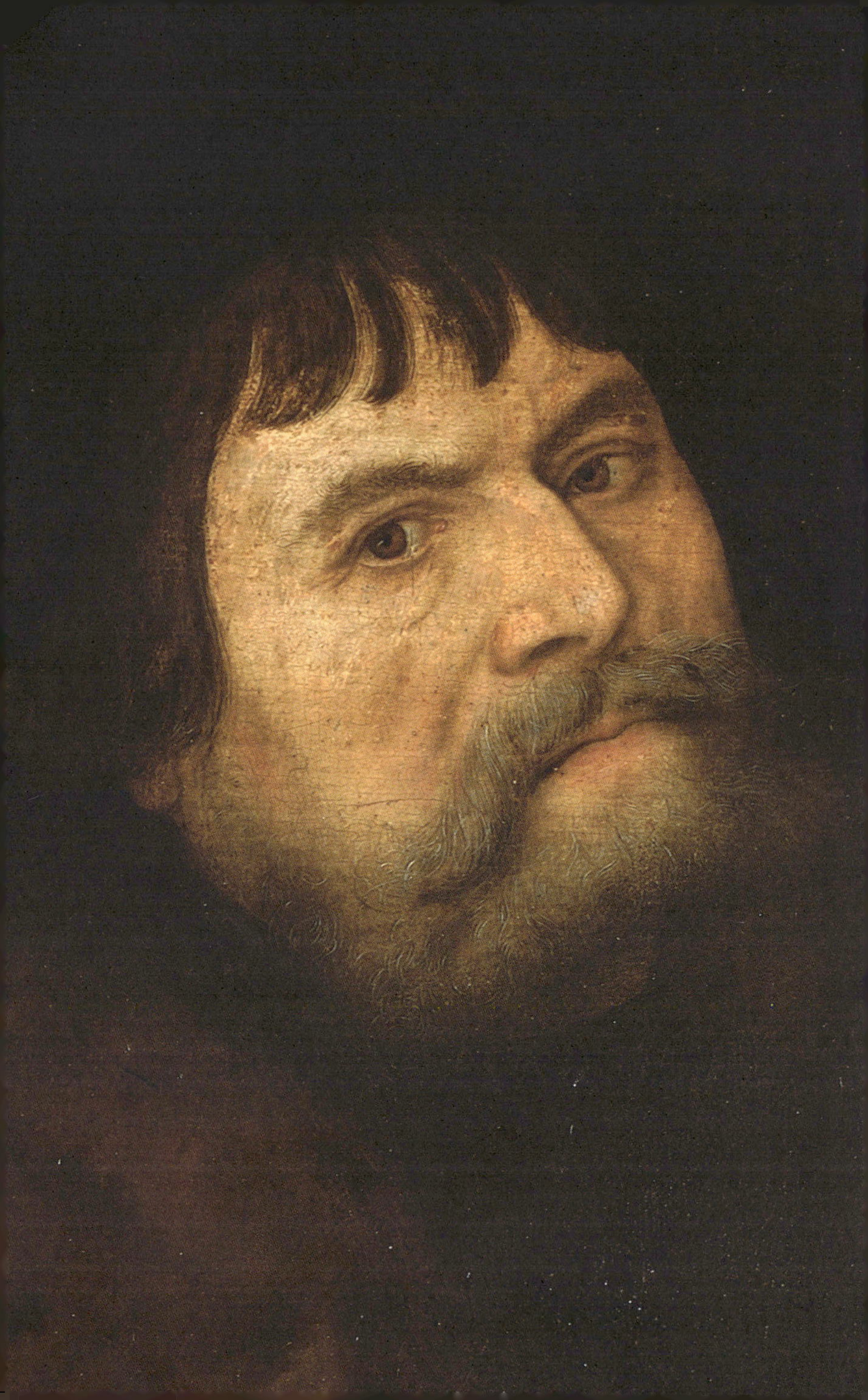

Cranach
A–Z

Teresa Präauer

Translated by Shaun Whiteside

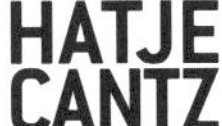

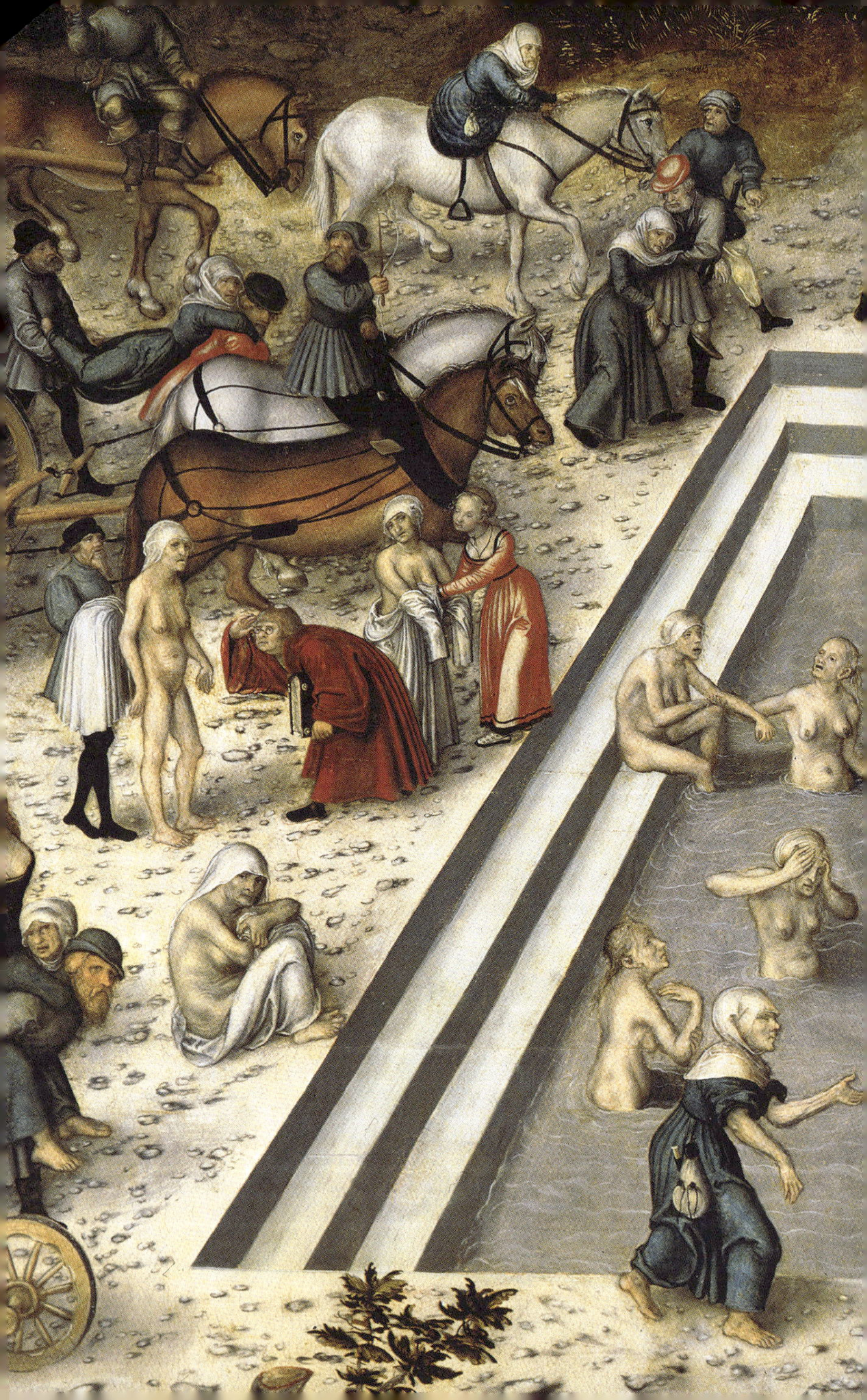

A → Ah, Cranach!

B → Bust of a Painter

C → Cranach Who?

D → Donors and Patrons

E → Eve

F → Force

G → Glad rags

H → Harpy

I → Instagrammability

J → Juvenescence

K → "Kassel" Brown

L → Luther

M → Monsters

N → Not the star

O → Ornament

P → Picasso

Q → Quire

R → Ruse

S → Scrapbook

T → Threat

U → Unsolved Mysteries

V → Venus

W → Website

XY → X-RaY

Z → Zooming in

The Golden Age ca. 1530
Wood 73.5 × 105.5 cm
Bayerische Staatsgemäldesammlungen,
Alte Pinakothek, Munich

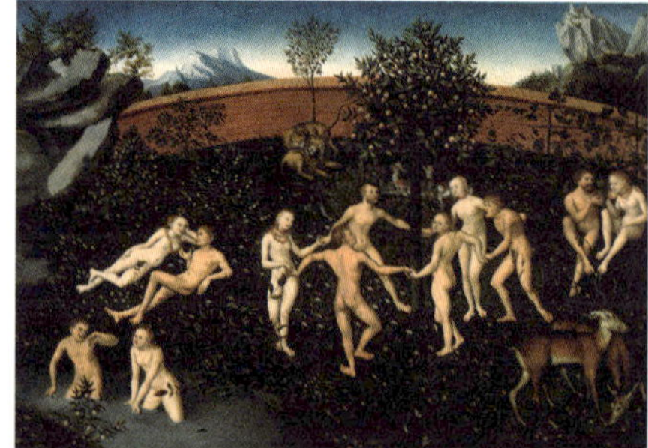

I would like to begin with this exclamation—
"Ah, Cranach!" For often have I stood in front
of Cranach's paintings and sighed "Cranach!"
That "Ah!" is prompted by the joy of looking at
a painting. There are people—and my readers are
bound to be among them—who are truly greedy
for paintings. They seek in them both beauty
and ugliness, an irritation of conventional seeing habits. We want to know the history of the
paintings and learn the stories in and behind
these paintings. Their colors, lines, and patterns,
the hands and the eyes, the space in them,
and the frame that encompasses the painting.

What I like so much about Cranach is his pictorial
language. Particularly that of the many little
naked men and women, who are painted so
smoothly and look a little like wax figures. They
swim, they dance through the Garden of Eden,
they contort their limbs, curl their fingers. Often
animals are placed beside them, ducking under
a bush or peering out from behind a tree. The
animals have round, gleaming eyes, while the
people often have almond eyes, a mild smile on
their narrow lips. Today this smile might appear
distant or even ironic to us. For me that is what
constitutes the gentle humor in Cranach's
paintings, whether or not the painter intended
it that way. I can't help grinning when I look
at that smile. That's why I love Cranach's paintings. Over the next few pages there will be a
few things to be said about his figures, motifs,
themes, and materials. Ah, Cranach!

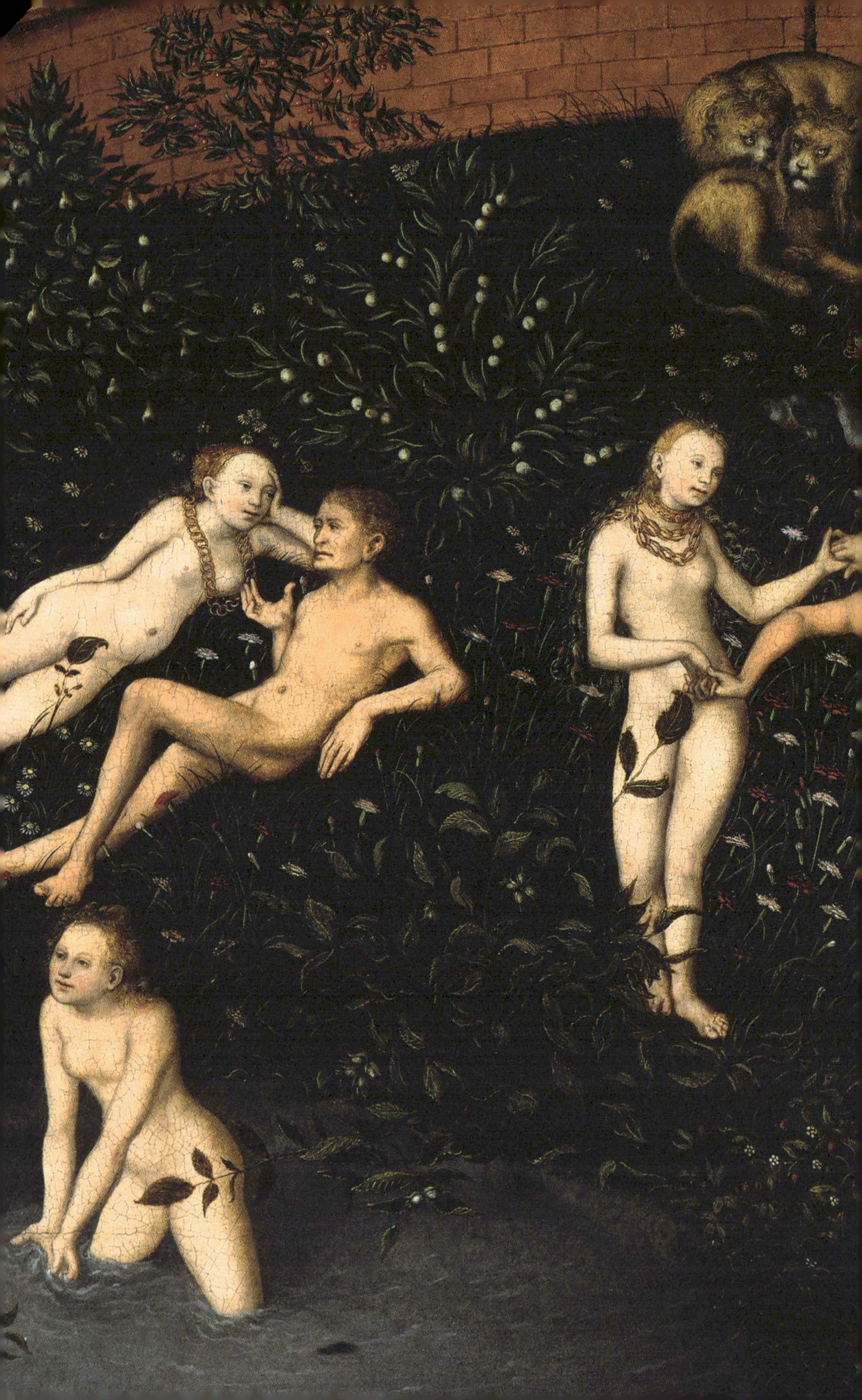

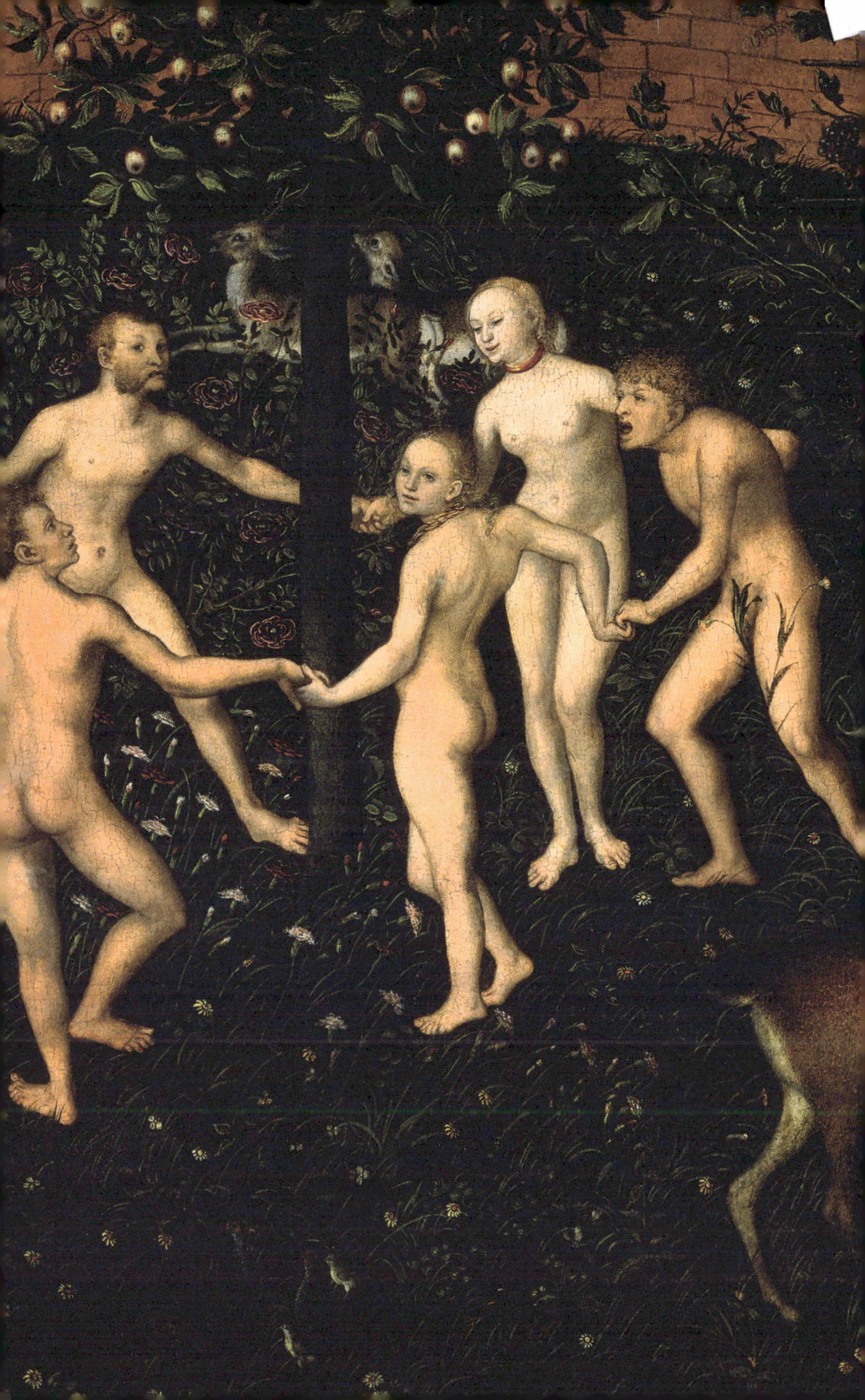

B→ Bust of a Painter

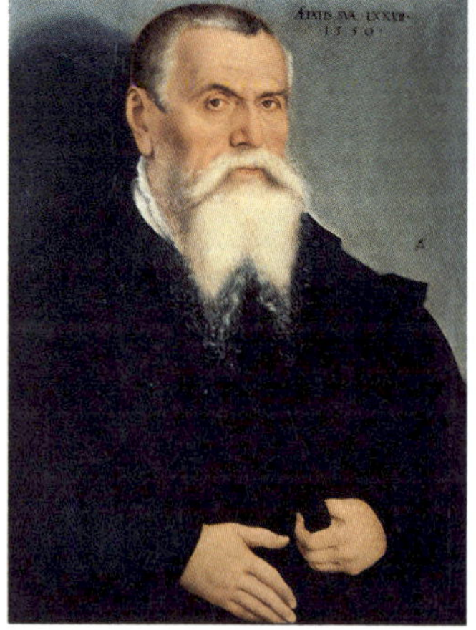

Lucas Cranach the Younger
Portrait of Lucas Cranach the Elder at Age 77
1550
Mixed media on wood 64 × 49 cm
Galleria degli Uffizi, Florence

A bust or half-length portrait shows a head and torso: only part of the sitter is shown, the rest is a mystery. The same applies to the painter Cranach. His first works can be dated to around 1500, by which time he was just thirty years old. Where had he lived before that, and what paintings had he made?

Lucas Cranach painted the *Crucifixion* and the first portraits known to us in Vienna which, with 20,000 inhabitants, was at the time one of the largest cities in the Holy Roman Empire and a center of early humanism. It was a time of transition: in following on from classical traditions, the Renaissance strove to break with the Middle Ages.

Lucas Cranach the Elder was born in 1472 in the Franconian town of Kronach. He learned the trade from his father Hans Möller and became a wandering apprentice. From this time on he chose the surname Cranach and signed his paintings with the initials "LC." Leaving one's place of origin meant choosing a new name—many artists continue to do the same today: the conductor Franz Welser-Möst is a Möst from Wels, the painter Christian Ludwig Attersee spent his youth on Lake Atter, and the French artist Niki de Saint Phalle—well no, apparently, that's the name she was born with.

The artistic profession as we know it today, and the self-image that went with it, were already beginning to form in Cranach's time. Henceforth it would no longer be the craft of the medieval picture-maker that occupied the center ground, but the culture and talents of the Renaissance man. In the portrait—a new type of painting— the commissioning patrons from an influential social class, the merchants and burghers of a city, are reflected. In a self-portrait the artist shows and questions himself as an individual.

Self-portraits of Cranach exist only as details within groups of figures. Probably the best-known portrait was painted on wood by his son Lucas Cranach the Younger in 1550. It shows his father, already aged seventy-seven, with a full white beard. Over his light-colored shirt he wears a black *schaube*—a wide-sleeved cloak which, with the beret, was considered essential humanist clothing. Cranach looks directly at us, and we gaze with admiration at the hands of a painter—they have painted thousands of pictures.

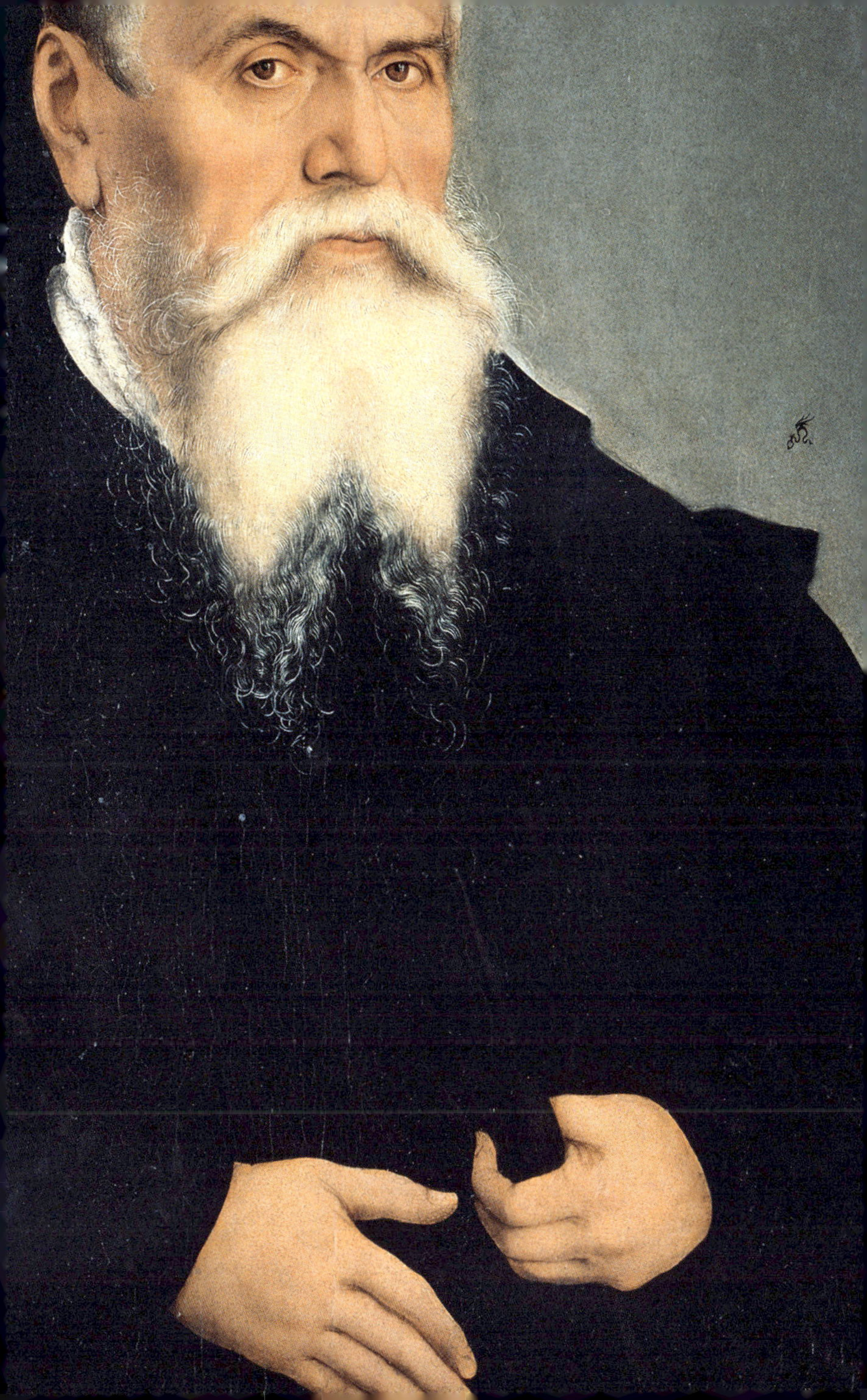

c → Cranach Who?

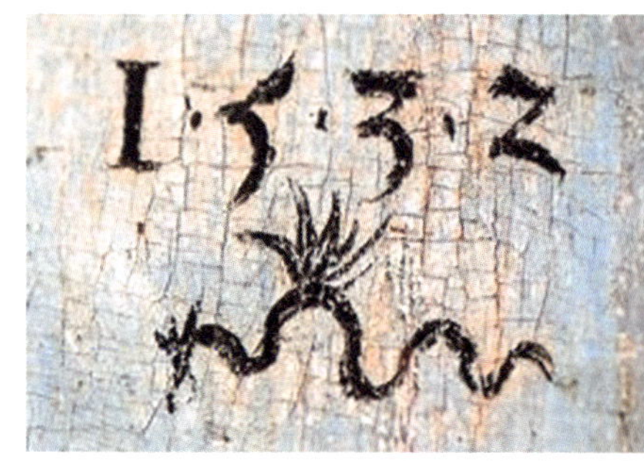

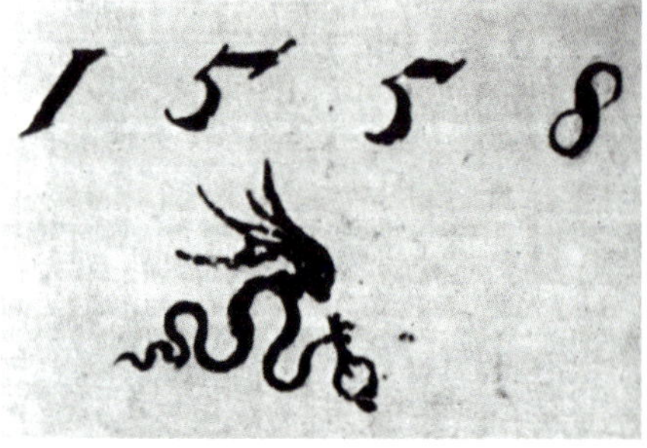

Detail with signature from
Johann the Constant 1532
Mixed media on wood 13.1 × 12.4 cm
Private collection

Detail with signature from
Lucas Cranach the Younger
Raising of Lazarus (Meyenburg Epitaph)
1558
Oil on wood 230 × 200 cm

When we speak of Cranach, we usually mean Lucas Cranach the Elder. But sometimes we also mean the Elder together with his workshop. And then again sometimes Cranach just means the Lucas Cranach workshop, which itself produced well-known masters. There are also the anonymous masters of the Cranach workshop, the wider "circle of Cranach." There are copies, and there are imitators who are also part of Cranach research. Then there is Lucas Cranach the Younger and his workshop, directly continuing his father's work. Finally, there is Lucas Cranach the Younger, who has only lately been rediscovered and valued as an artist in his own right, not least in distinction from his father. There are precise date limits, there are material analyses, and sometimes there are mere assumptions concerning attributions. In the case of some paintings, it is hard to say who exactly painted them. Some were made on the principle of the division of labor, while in some instances the master and workshop leader made the preparatory designs, and perhaps checked the painting in the end and completed one last detail.

It is probably also in line with the workshop model to see the entire oeuvre as the work of several hands. In this respect Cranach is something like a traditional craft business, and at the same time a modern "Factory" like the one we know from Andy Warhol: it's assembled by apprentices, pupils and masters, mingling with party people and the smart-set sitters.

Anything that left Cranach's workshop was given the Cranach emblem, a kind of logo or branding, which he was given in 1508 along with a heraldic letters patent. It shows a snake with erect wings, the precise description of which is almost poetic in tone: "[…] a black serpent, having in the middle two black bat wings, on its head a red crown and in its mouth a golden ring studded with a ruby and on its shield a helmet with a black and a yellow helmet cover, and on the helmet a yellow circlet wound round with thorns […]." After the death in 1537 of his first-born son Hans, who fell ill on a study tour to Italy and subsequently died of a fever, the snake lowers its wings and the symbol changes.

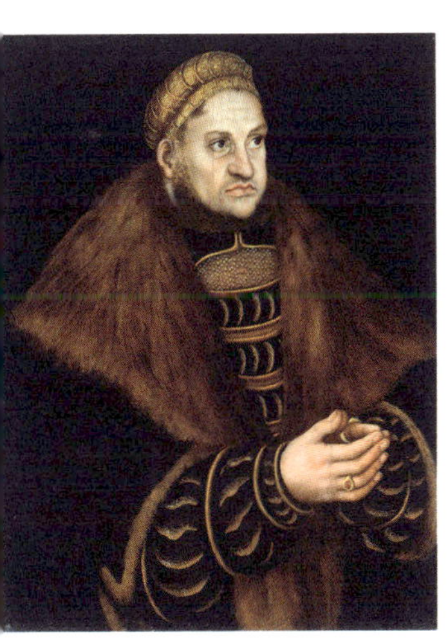

*Frederick III (The Wise) Elector
of Saxony* ca. 1515
Oil on coniferous wood 64.4 × 50.1 cm
Art collection of the Veste Coburg

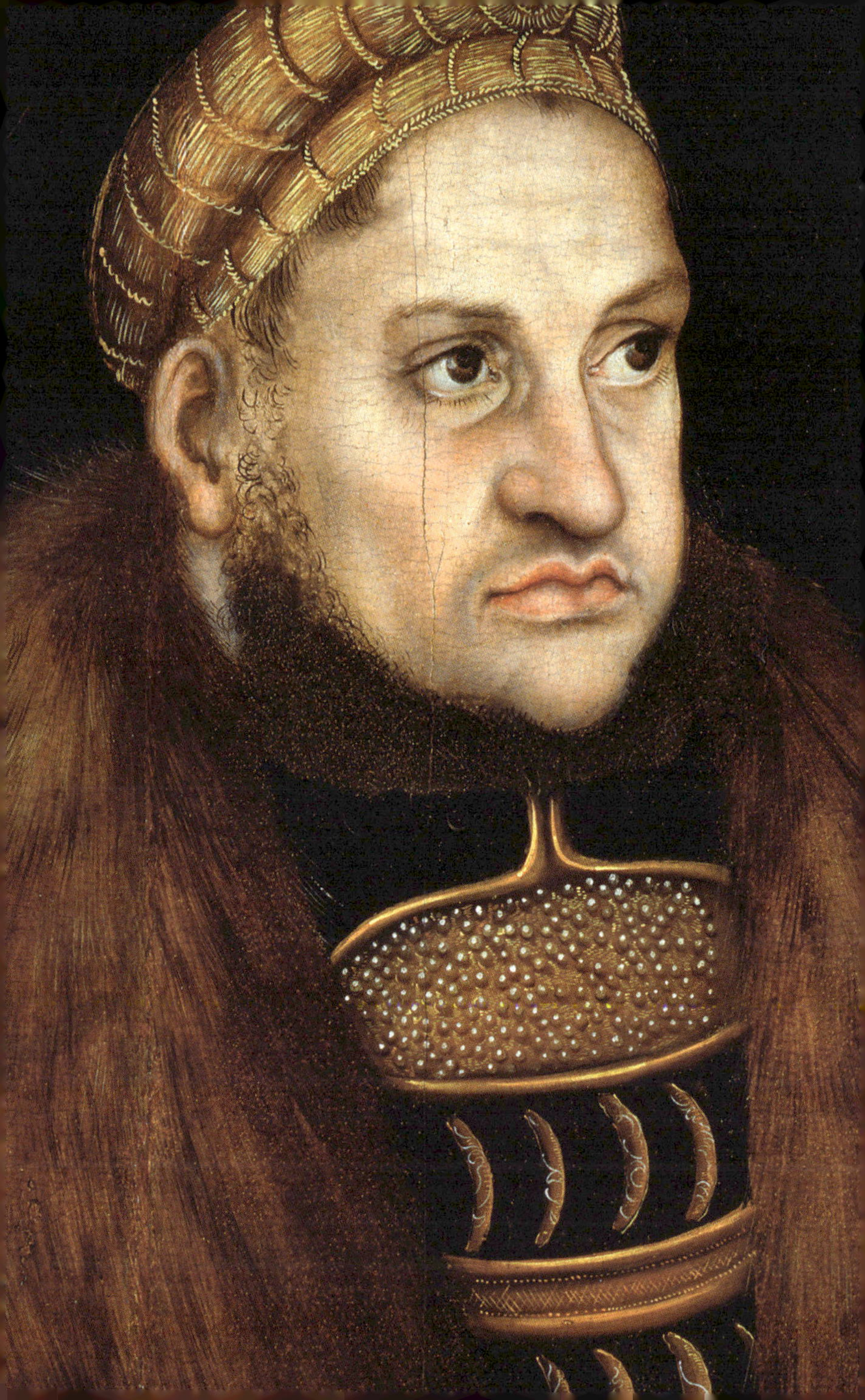

Cranach is also not easy to pin down in terms of his employers. From 1505, he was court painter to the Frederick the Wise Elector of Saxony, in the royal capital of Wittenberg, and retained the post under his successors John the Steadfast and John Frederick the Magnanimous. After the deposition of the latter in 1550, Cranach the Elder followed him to Augsburg, and later to Innsbruck and Weimar. He had already transferred the management of the workshop to his son. We find numerous portraits of the Wise, the Steadfast, and even the Magnanimous in the work of the Cranachs—they thus established the Saxon-Thuringian court style.

The picture *Frederick III (The Wise) Elector of Saxony* (ca. 1515) shows the prince praying with hands folded. The panel has been liberated from a set of altarpieces and shows us that holders of worldly power still quite self-evidently had their place within the sacred space of the painting. Frederick the Wise, a Catholic throughout his lifetime, supported the reformer Martin Luther; Cranach's paintings, as well as being a re-presentation of the establishment, also testify to the social upheavals of the time. At the same time, he also made numerous paintings for a Catholic opponent of Luther, Cardinal Albrecht of Brandenburg. Cranach lived in a time when panel painting was both flourishing and in crisis. There was iconoclasm and the accompanying destruction of paintings, there were prohi-bitions on images and changes to forms of representation: inscriptions were defaced, but at the same time new pictorial motifs were developed in close exchange with humanists and reformers. Today Cranach is seen as a pictorial innovator straddling the Middle Ages and the beginning of the modern age, his repertoire containing both mythological and biblical themes, devoted both to naturalistic depiction and pictorial invention.

Frederick the Wise collected relics and owned thousands of them, of which Cranach documented a small part, bound in a kind of inventory catalogue, the Wittenberg Relic Book, or *Wittenberger Heiltumsbuch*. Among the relics in question are thorns, bones, nails, wood shavings, locks of hair, clothes, torture instruments, sandals, rings, and ashes. One had only to touch or even merely gaze upon the relic to be absolved of one's sins for a few days. Luther turned a mocking eye on the trade in and reverence for relics, but also points out that we already have a relic, "the Word of our Lord"—the message of a not quite so worldly donor.

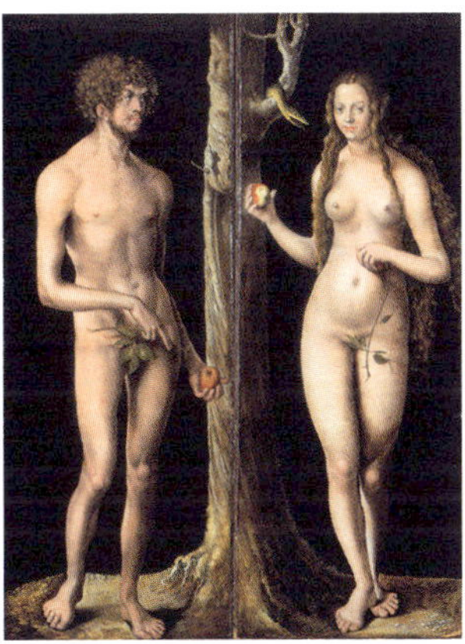

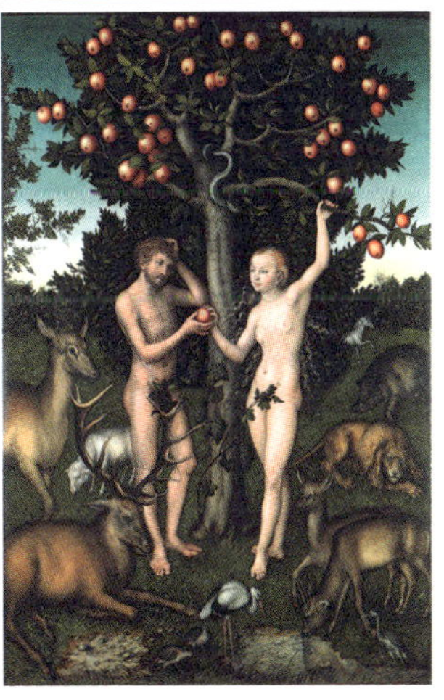

Adam and Eve ca. 1508–1510
Mixed media on beech wood
139 × 53.9 cm each
Musée des Beaux-Arts et D'Archéologie
Besançon

Adam and Eve 1526
Oil on maple wood 117 × 80 cm
University of London,
Courtauld Institute of Art

Because the biblical Eve was intellectually bored in Paradise, she plucked the apple from the Tree of Knowledge. Within Cranach's lifetime there were several such pluckings of the apple which would have a lasting effect on the way the world was seen. With the invention of book printing and a new social class striving to achieve influence, the Church's monopoly on culture was also toppled.

When Cranach was twenty, Columbus sailed for India and ended up in the Bahamas. In 1518, Magellan set off on a circumnavigation of the world, which thereafter was no longer flat but round. Only two decades later, with Copernicus, this globe was no longer at the center of the universe but revolved along with other planets around the sun. Travel sketches from a "New World" also extended Cranach's pictorial world. An animal like the grey parrot from the *Portrait of Cardinal Albrecht of Brandenburg as Saint Jerome in his Study* from 1526, from the European perspective, represents one of those discoveries.

Albrecht Dürer in Nuremberg and Lucas Cranach in Wittenberg were the most significant painters of the period north of the Alps, and were mentioned together with Albrecht Altdorfer, Hans Baldung Grien, Matthias Grünewald, and Hans Holbein. As contemporaries they were colleagues and rivals, each was familiar with some of the work of the other, and they reacted to one another in their paintings. In this painterly

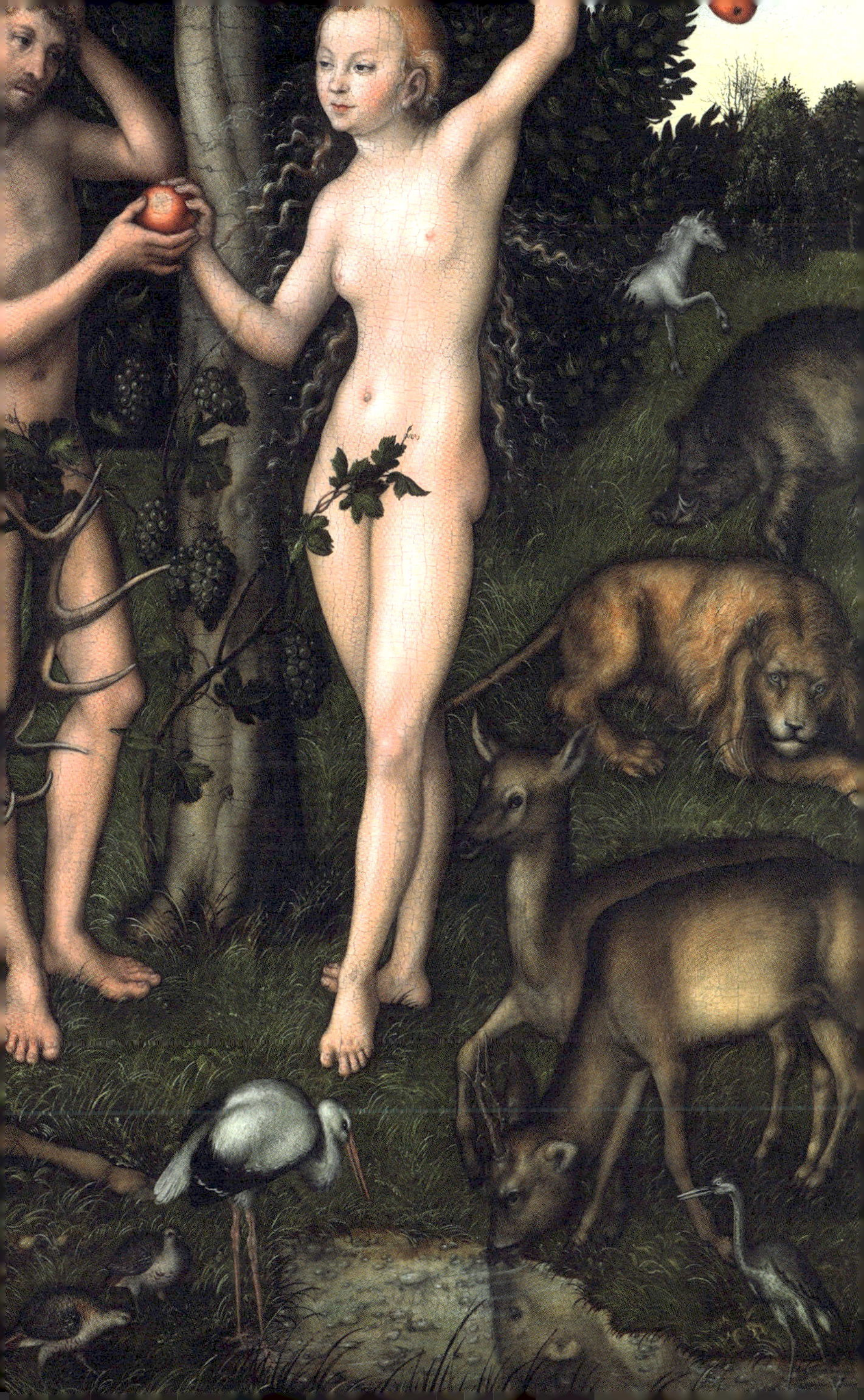

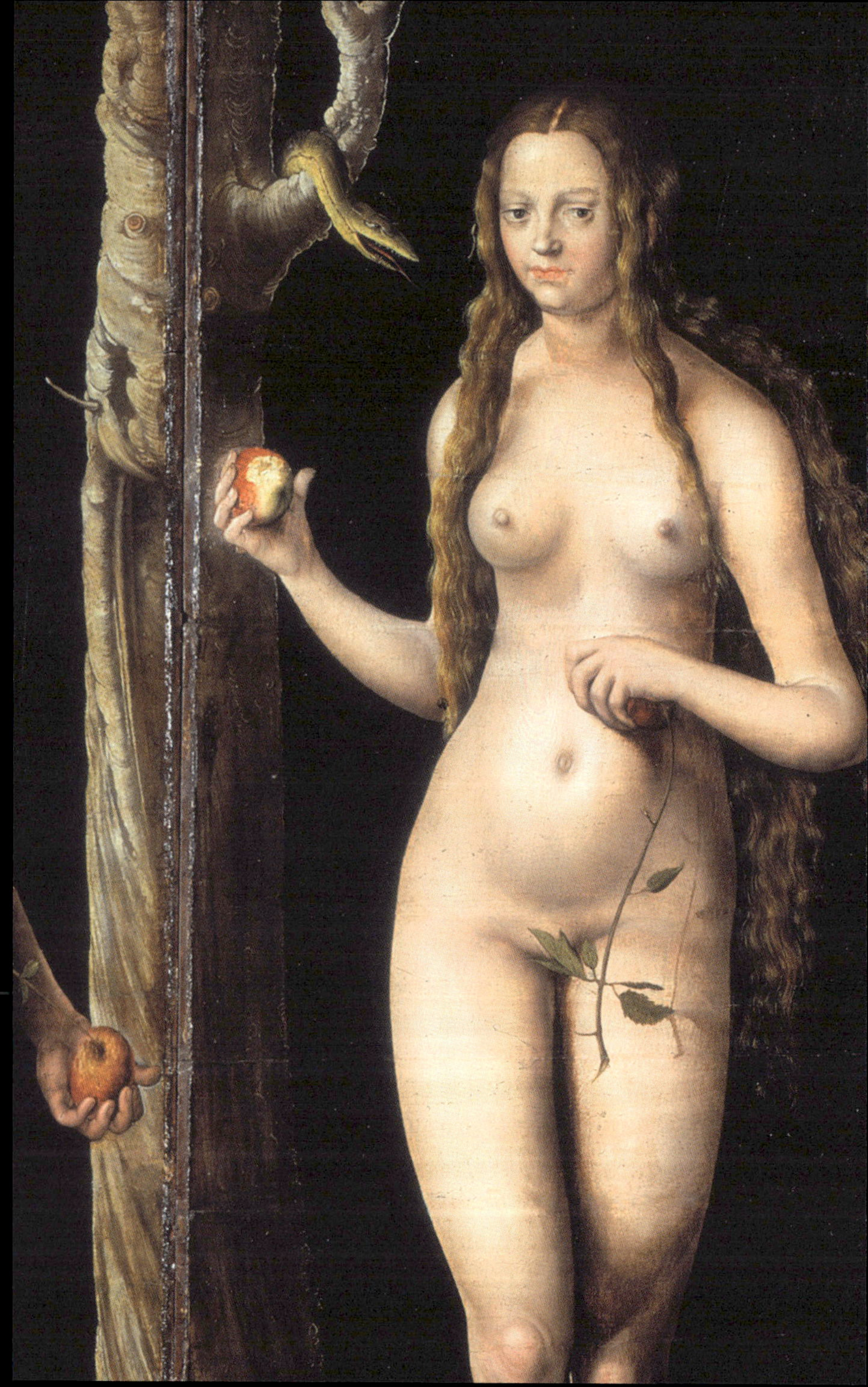

competition Cranach also resorted to foul play: it has been shown that he predated some of his woodcuts to lay claim to the invention of pictorial subjects.

Two works made in dialogue with models established by Dürer were Cranach's *Adam and Eve* dating from between 1508 and 1510, two panels connected in the middle by a tree-trunk attached to a branch with a snake. This was a pictorial invention of Dürer's. The two figures resemble classical statues, life-sized, free-standing against a monochrome background, their bodies idealized and stylized. The pair have also elegantly mastered the art of holding a leafy twig in front of their bodies to conceal their genitals. Dürer's couple looks sweet and youthful, while in Cranach the features are individual and lifelike, and the expressions of the two first humans are also rather fierce: Adam is looking at the snake, while Eve has already bitten into the apple and looks us in the eye. Cranach painted the motif repeatedly in different variations, and we are tempted into looking at them all.

F → Force

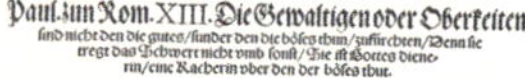
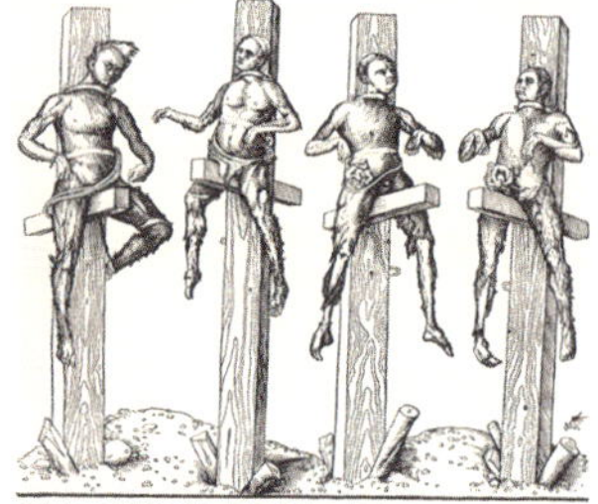

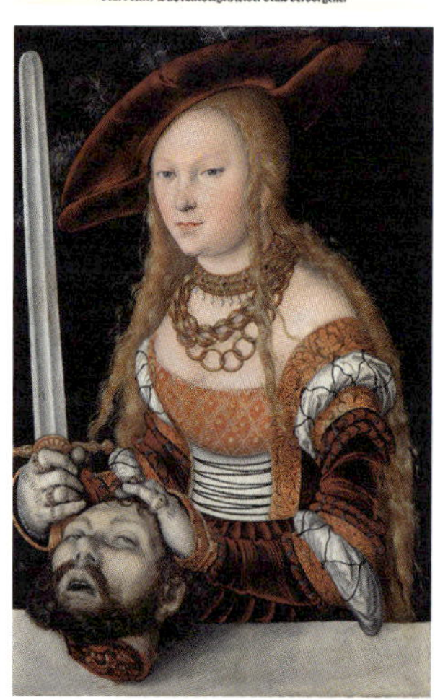

Lucas Cranach the Younger
Burning of Witches in Wittenberg 1540
Woodcut

Judith with the Head of Holofernes ca. 1530
Limewood 87.7 × 58.1 cm
Kunsthistorisches Museum Vienna,
Picture Gallery

The sixteenth century in Europe was not only
the heyday of humanism but also a time of force
and violence as a consequence of changes
of rule, wars of faith, peasants' rebellions, and
epidemics of the plague. The hail and storms
of the Little Ice Age led to failed harvests, famine,
and price rises in trade.

Consequently, Cranach's paintings are also
full of executions, flagellations and beheadings.
Full of mockeries, crucifixions, lamentations,
temptations, torture, martyrdoms. Death and
devils, demons and werewolves, fighting and
wailing, men of sorrow and the fall from grace.

One woodcut by Cranach the Younger shows a
witch-burning about to take place of four people
in Wittenberg, giving 1 May 1540 as the date
on the flyer. They have plainly been tortured
beforehand, and now we see their torn clothes,
their wounds, and their innards. They are nailed
to wooden posts, their faces appear to be sleeping, their limbs stiff and distorted. They are
accused of consorting with the devil, magic, and
the making of poisonous powder.

Estimates of the numbers of witch persecutions
and trials in Europe during this time are in
the millions; tens of thousands in the German-
speaking world alone, the majority of the victims
were women. In his woodcut, Cranach does
not criticize the process, but rather documents
it as for a newspaper report. Perhaps we might

prefer to turn to a female avenger whom Lucas Cranach the Elder painted in many different variations—*Judith with the Head of Holofernes*. Judith wears the fashion of the time as we know it from the wardrobe of the Saxon princesses. She wears her hair down and holds a sword in her right hand. The head of the enemy general has been severed, his skin is already pale, his huge wound faces towards us.

Judith has a long tradition in paintings in art history. She is on the one hand the devout forerunner of Mary, and on the other a powerful Protestant opponent in the defensive alliance of individual princes and cities of the Empire against the Catholic Emperor Charles V. Violence is not apparent in the figure of Judith herself, but only in the severed head of the slaughtered Holofernes. Judith wears a barely perceptible smile, and her leather gloves remain clean and white.

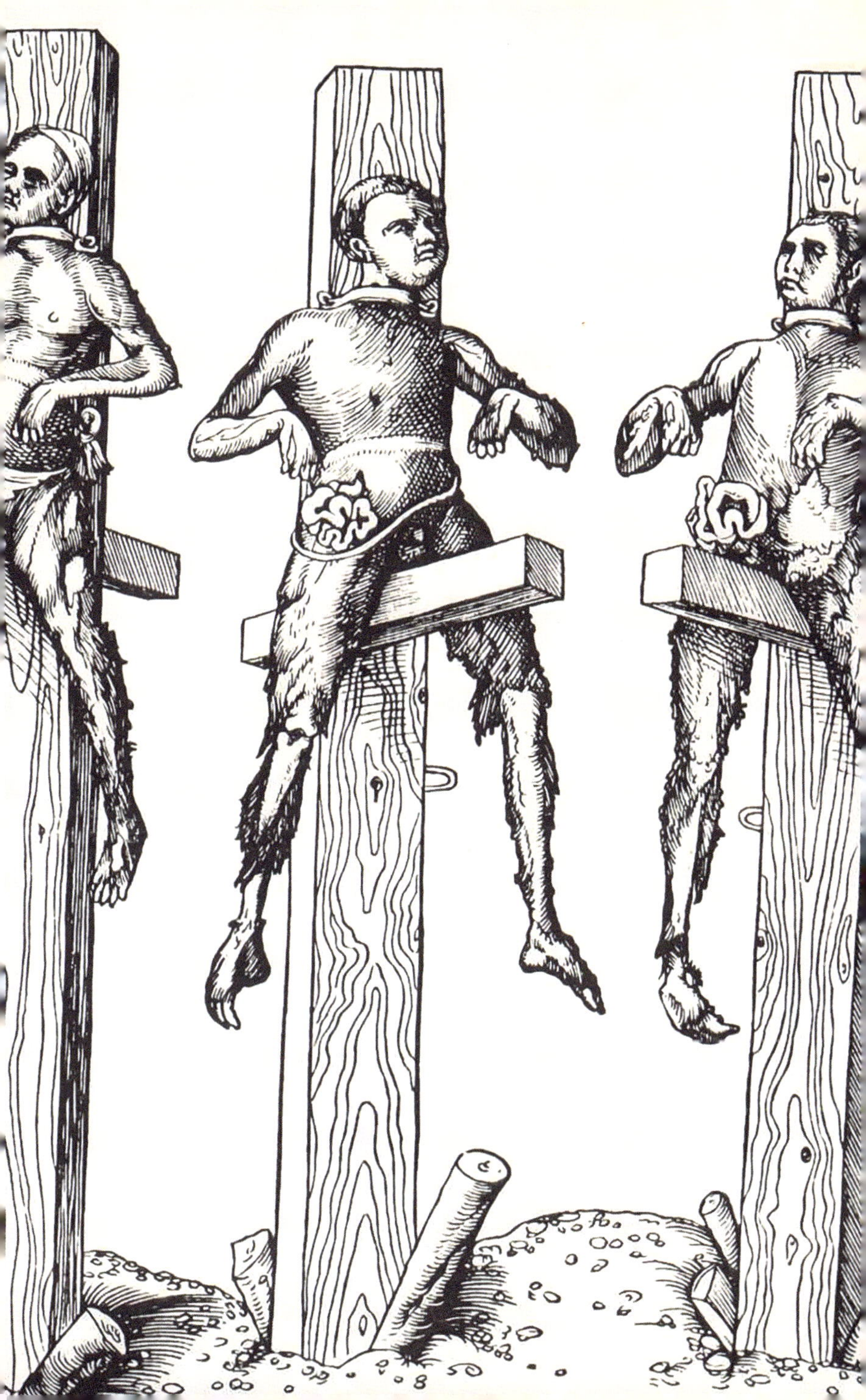

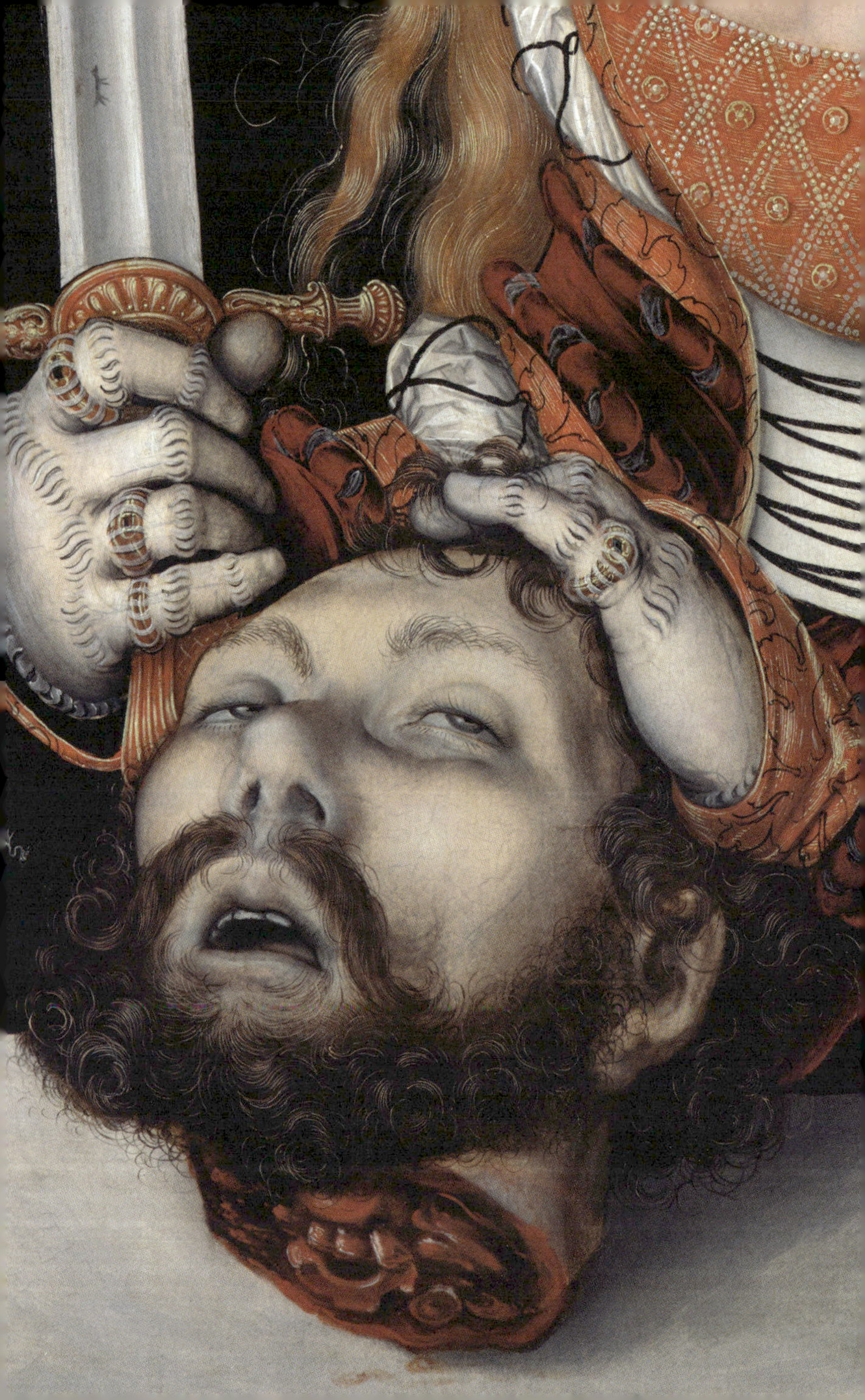

G → Glad rags

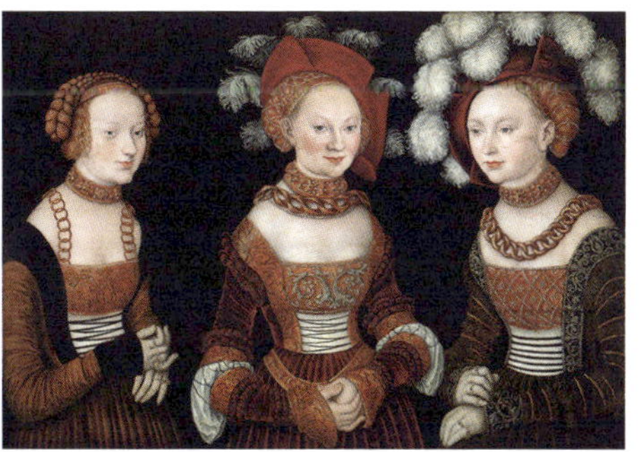

The Princesses Sibylla (1515–1592),
Emilia (1516–1591) and Sidonia of Saxony
(1518–1575) ca. 1535
Lime wood 62 × 89 cm
Kunsthistorisches Museum Vienna,
Picture Gallery

Cranach's dressing-up box is full to bursting: chains, hats, shirts, and coats are displayed in his paintings as attributes of wealth. Our cover model is Princess Emilia of Saxony, just nineteen and married for two years to the margrave of Brandenburg-Ansbach, George the Pious (both, incidentally, were early devotees of Luther). Lucas Cranach the Younger painted two posthumous pictures of George: a fat, black-clad colossus of a man, once with his decorated beret on his head, once in his hand.

Emilia can be seen alongside her sisters in the painting *The Princesses Sibylla, Emilia and Sidonia of Saxony*. It hangs in the Kunsthistorisches Museum in Vienna, and a note regarding the work in an inventory from 1619 has been preserved: "*Drei weibsbildnus fon Krunacher, gar lebhaftig*," ("Three portraits of women by Krunacher, most quick.")

The princesses wear elaborately braided hair with pearled hairbands and hairnets, and red berets with opulent feathers. They wear ribbon collars studded with stones and pearls around their necks, rings flash from under slit leather gloves, and the skin of their décolleté is covered with gold chains so heavy and so bling that they would arouse the envy of rappers from present-day music videos.

Emilia is the only one to wear a delicately pleated, sheer blouse over her deep décolleté, and the narrowness of her shoulders is emphasized, her bodice tied tightly, while the skirt below the waist spreads wide again, and extravagant slit sleeves cover her arms.

When we read today about the later lives of the three princesses, we find separations, accusations of poisoning and involvement in witch trials. But here we see them smiling softly and wittily, and really "most quick."

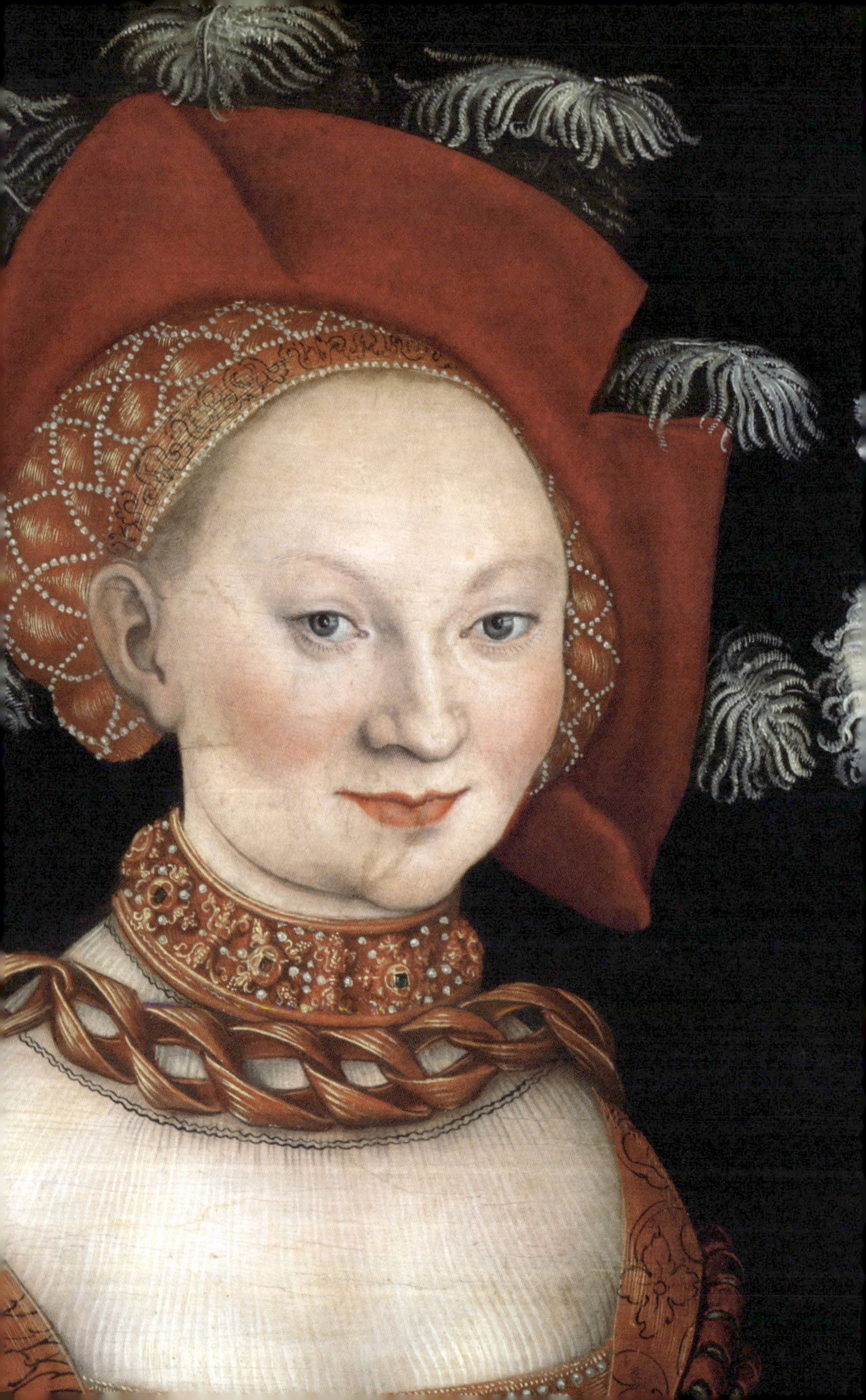

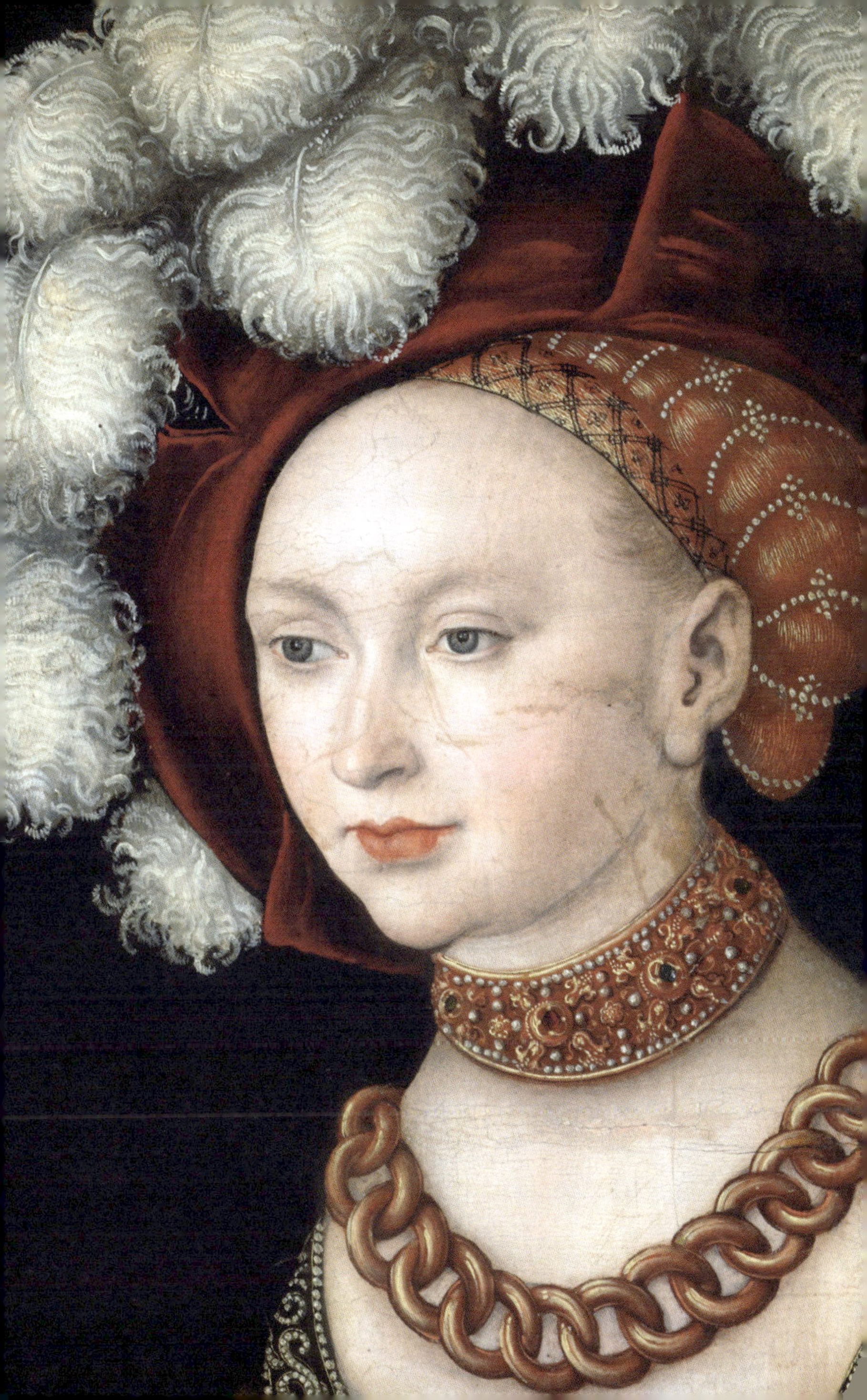

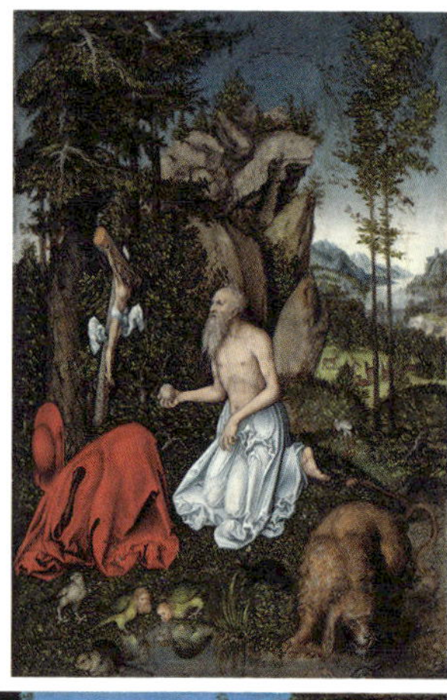

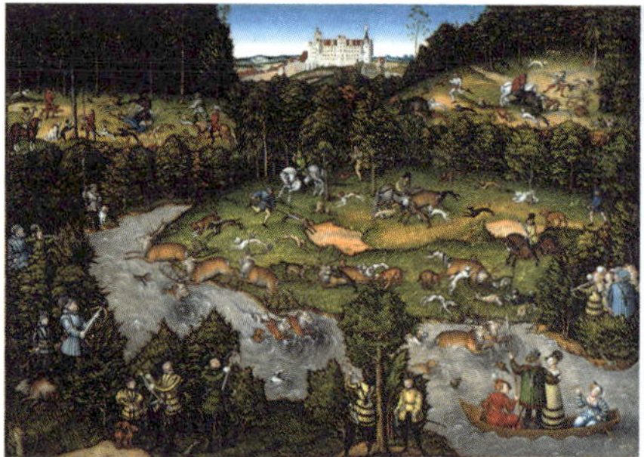

Saint Jerome ca. 1525
Oil on fir wood 89.8 × 66.5 cm
Tiroler Landesmuseum, Innsbruck

Hunting near Hartenfels Castle 1540
Oil, originally on wood, transferred
to masonite 116.8 × 170.2 cm
Cleveland Museum of Art

In Greek mythology the harpy is a hybrid of human and bird, and we still encounter her quite matter-of-factly in nature studies until well into the Early Modern age. Painters liked to use pattern books for their depictions of flora and fauna, in which plants and animals were collected and represented in the form of woodcuts or engravings. What Cranach knew from his immediate experience he painted in exactly the same way as the unknown and invented animals from the pattern books, so long as their existence had not been convincingly refuted. In one of Cranach's many depiction of this episode, Saint Jerome kneels in the woods by a small pond, barely larger than a puddle, doing penance for his impious preoccupation with the writings of antiquity. Two green birds with human faces crouch by the water's edge, one with a beard and one with feminine features and curly hair, which bends down and, as if it too must do penance, looks at its reflection. At the same time, to modern eyes the two harpies look very cute and comical, belying their murderous natures.

In addition to the harpies, animals are scattered around as if in a picture puzzle: we discover eagles, lizards, beavers, tortoises, pheasants, butterflies, squirrels, storks, and deer. Cranach is the painter of animals: of magpies, foxes, rabbits and roosters; of herons, sheep and cranes, of swans, ducks and bears, cows and unicorns. They dwell in Paradise and each have their own symbolic significance. But they also

provide an account, as in his many depictions
of hunting deer, of how animals are handled
by a court painter who has to accompany court
on the hunt. As if in a picture story, he shows
the sequences of the hunt, setting off on horse-
back, then rounding up the deer with hounds.
Pen-and-ink drawings of wild boar have been
preserved, along with *Two Dead Waxwings
Hanging on a Nail*, painted around 1530 in water-
color on paper. The animals in these paintings
often look at us directly, or else they are in eye
contact with the people in the paintings. Their
eyes are as big as the eyes of children, dark and
gleaming.

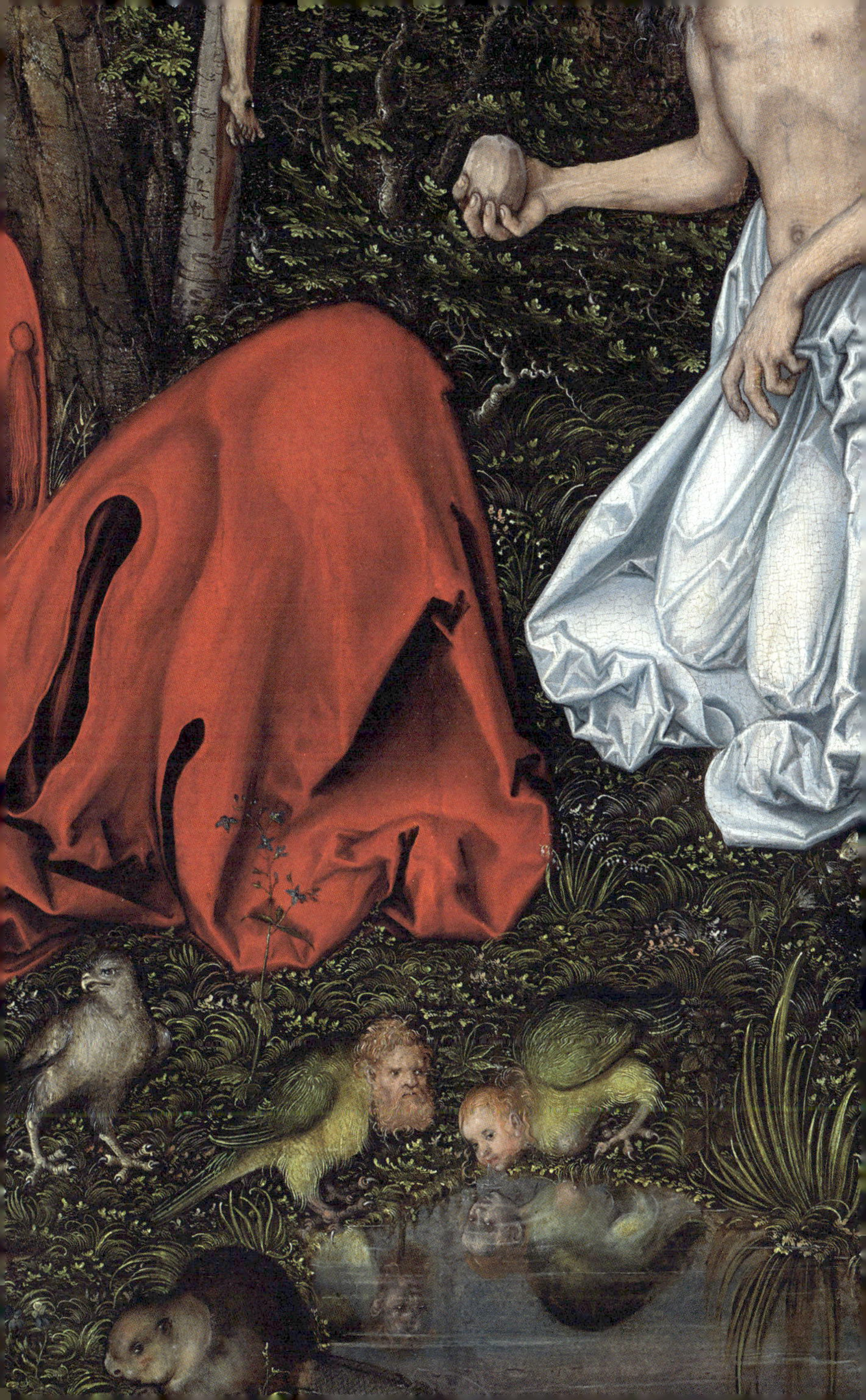

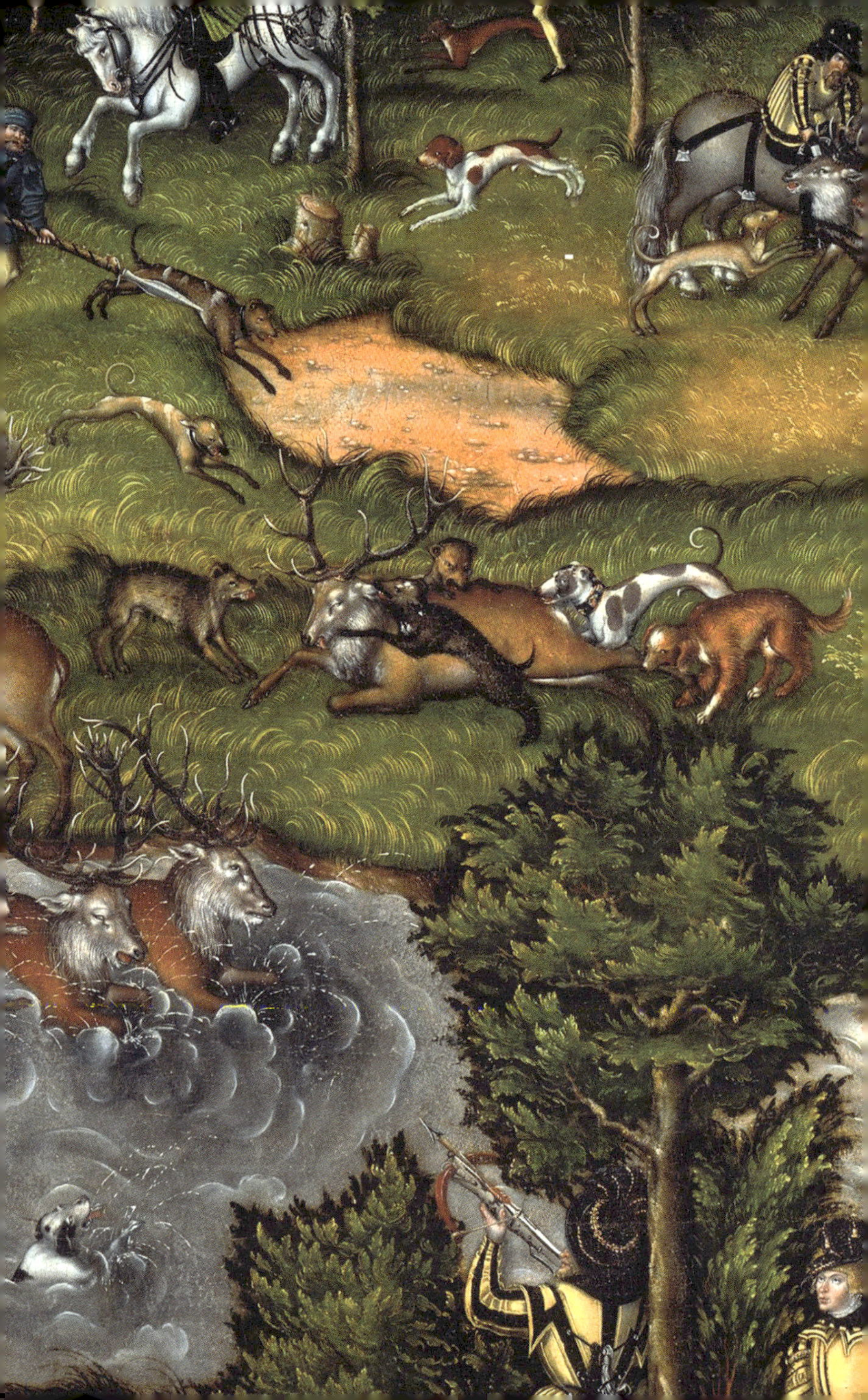

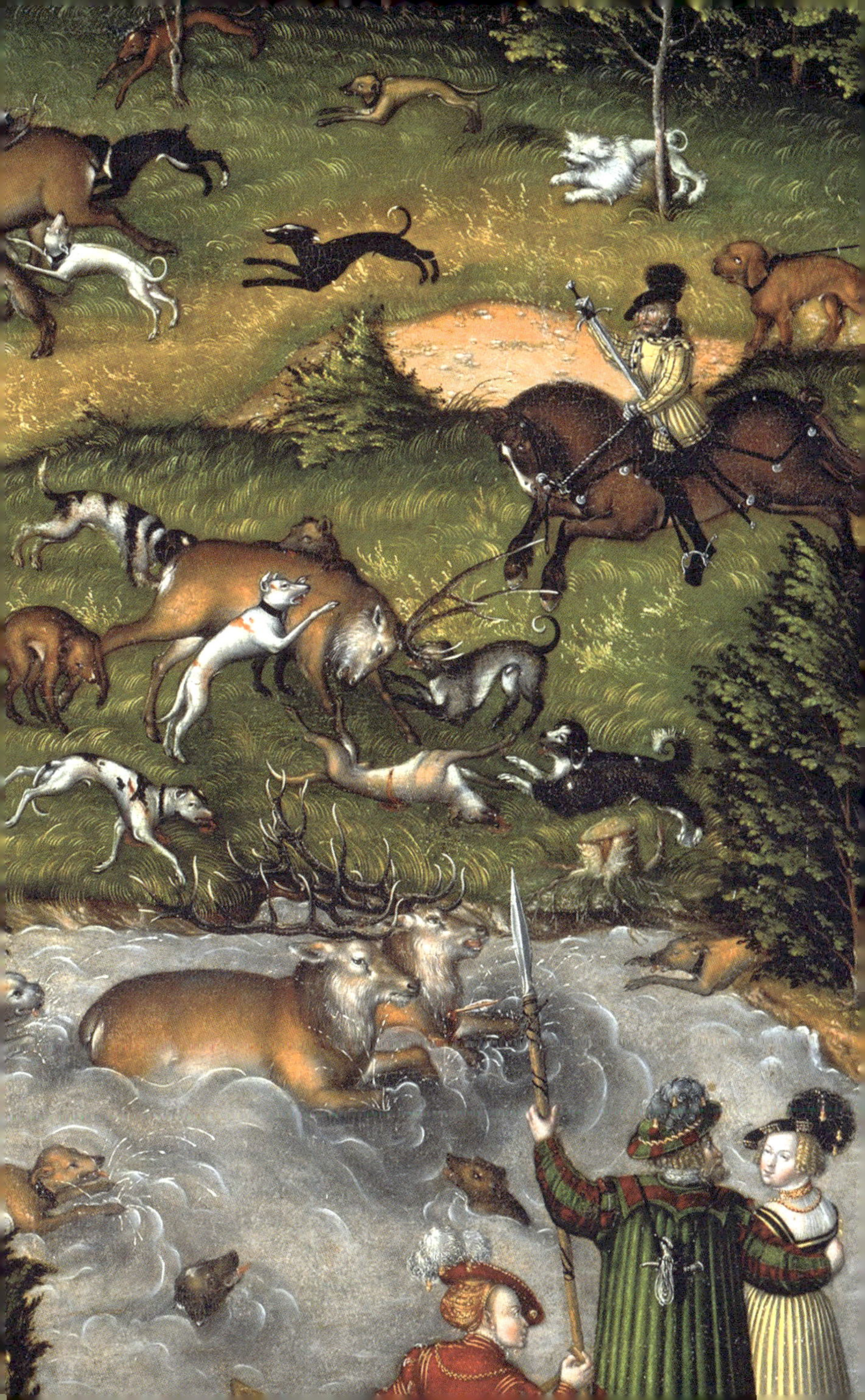

↦ Instagrammability

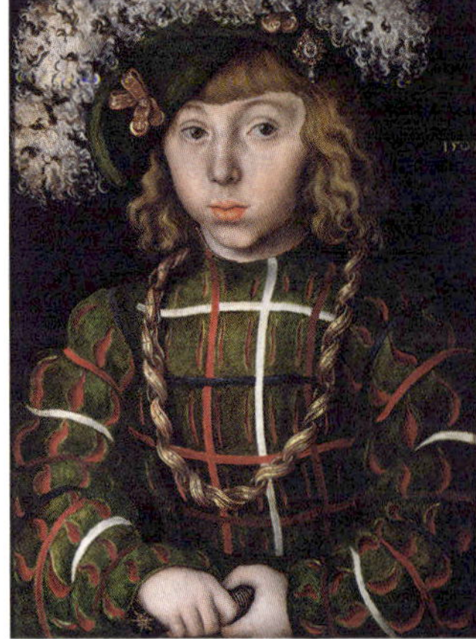

Portrait of Johann Friedrich the Magnanimous
Part of the diptych:
Two Electors of Saxony 1509
Oil on wood 42 × 31.2 cm
National Gallery, London

What photograph is interesting and attractive enough to be uploaded on to a digital platform and attract attention in the social network? What angle, what crop, what light and what filters favor the "Instagrammability" of the people, spaces, and objects thus depicted?

Cranach's figures with their perfect skin and stylized physical forms, narrow shoulders and little bellies, are perhaps not so far from the prettified portraits on the internet in the twenty-first century. His painter colleague, Albrecht Dürer, took a greater interest in anatomy, Cranach in stylizations: the round faces, the pointed chins, the narrow noses, the delicate mouths. The diagonal almond eyes, the strawberry-blonde curly hair, the relaxed features. The soft smiles of the women, directed at many of his male figures, for example in the depictions of Paradise and the Golden Age.

Instagram posts under the hashtag #lucascranach reveal Cranach graffiti, collages, ceramics, and costumes as well as private snapshots from museums of Eve, Judith, Luther and Katharina. They also include the pretty portrait of a little boy, *Portrait of Johann Friedrich the Magnanimous*, (John Frederick the Magnanimous), the son of John the Steadfast. It was originally part of a diptych: six-year-old John Frederick is shown here in place of his mother. She would have occupied the space within the "marriage portrait" had she not died giving birth to her son. John

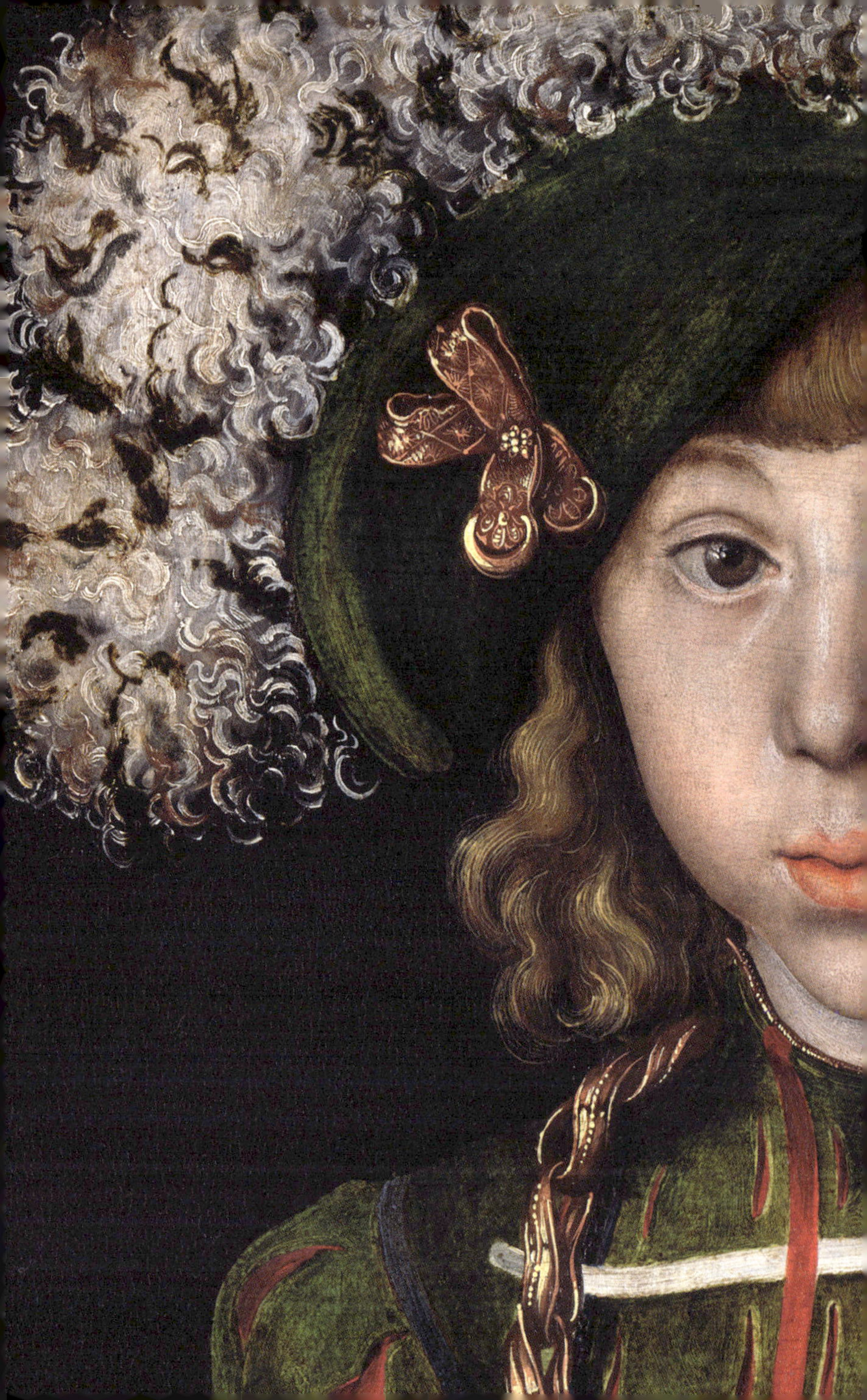

Frederick wears festive clothes, a green cap with ostrich feathers and a small amount of jewelry, and if a cat were sitting on his lap his popularity on Instagram could hardly be greater.

Another popular painting by Cranach on the online platform is *Lucretia*, alongside the note "sold at Christie's in New York for five million dollars." Following the fantasies of painters, seemingly no one could die more charmingly than Lucretia, who took her own life after being raped. In Cranach's painting we see her before she puts her plan into operation: naked except for a fur coat over her shoulders. In other variants she also wears a thin cloth around her body. She holds the sword to her breast as if playing with an ostrich feather.

Incidentally, photographs of female nipples must be retouched when published on Instagram—paintings are generously exempt from this.

J→ Juvenescence

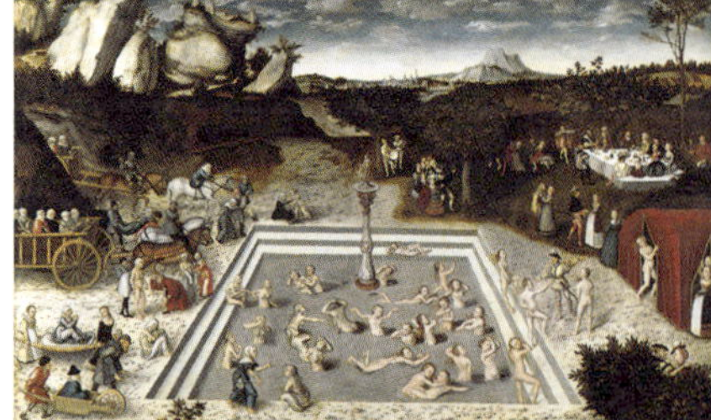

The Fountain of Youth 1546
Oil on wood 121 × 184 cm
Staatliche Museen zu Berlin,
Gemäldegalerie

When Lucas Cranach the Elder painted the *Fountain of Youth*, he was himself already seventy-four years old. Perhaps he even wished he could bathe in such a fountain—at any rate its design suggests a vivid imagination. We see the depth of a landscape, with cliffs and mountains in the background, and a fortified city. The sky is blue and covered with little clouds. Presented with strict central perspective and placed in the middle is a swimming pool into which lead three steps and, at its center, a fountain with statuettes of Venus and Cupid. On one side old women are being brought to the fountain, sitting in carriages, on stretchers, and in wheel-barrows. They wear coats and headscarves, they disrobe, and we see their old, naked bodies as they step into the water. They bathe, they swim, they scrub themselves. Their hair regains its reddish-blonde color, their skin loses its greyness, their bodies become young again. So, they climb back out of the pool and are received by oh-so noble gentlemen—who have, we hope, also had a good bath—and who now dress them again and invite them to a feast. One pair hide behind a bush, he with his arm around her shoulder. Life begins again, almost from the beginning. Tribulation, suffering, and disappointment have been washed away.

The bathers and swimmers in Cranach's work are always particularly charming and cheerful. In the representations of the Golden Age they swim in pairs, their bodies half covered

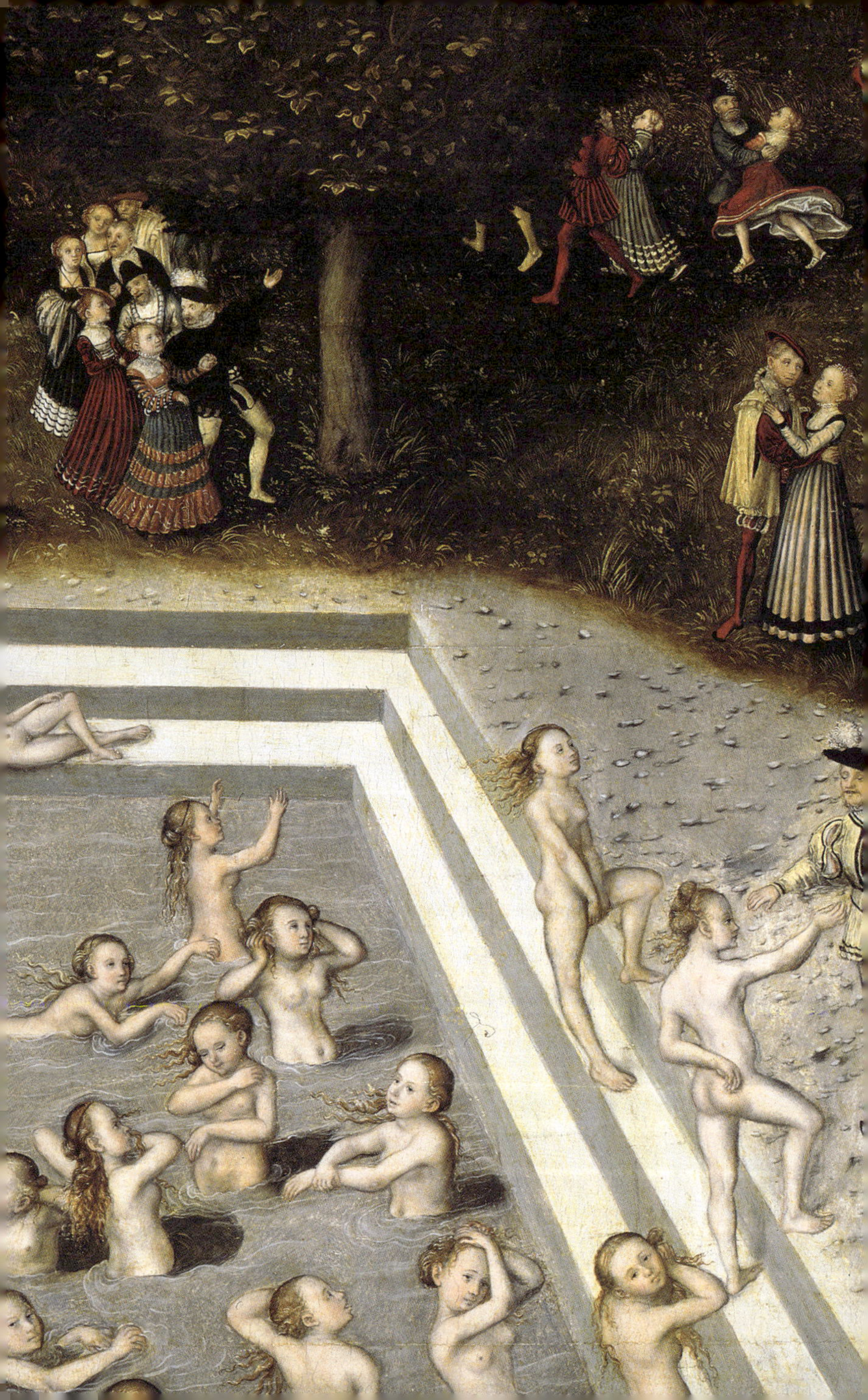

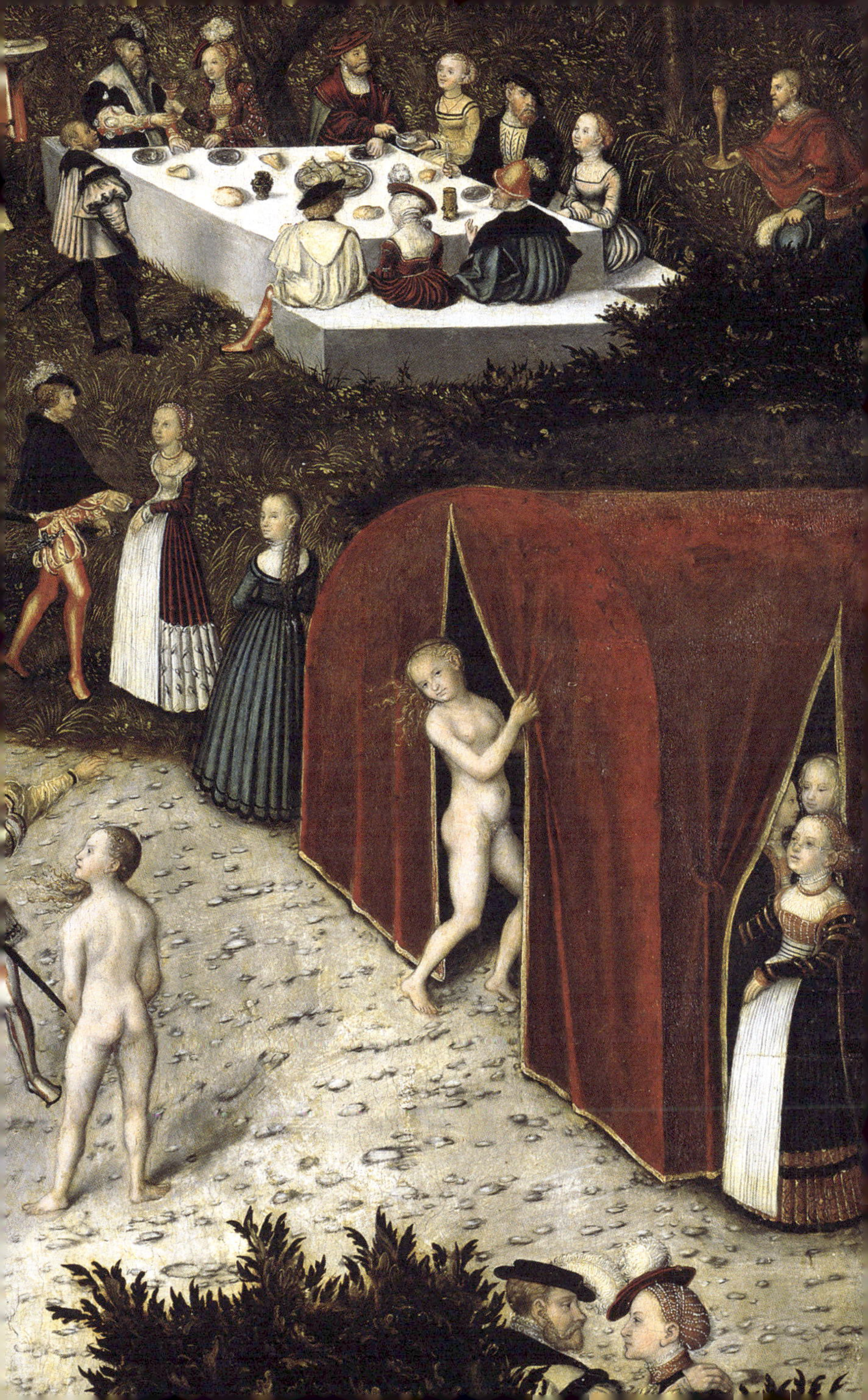

with water, half with their limbs upstretched in prancing, distorted movements. The spray of water itself produces beautiful scenes, which we can observe in the *Hunt at the Castle of Torgau in Honour of Charles V*, a busy puzzle of barking dogs and deer among the waves of the river.

K→ "Kassel" Brown

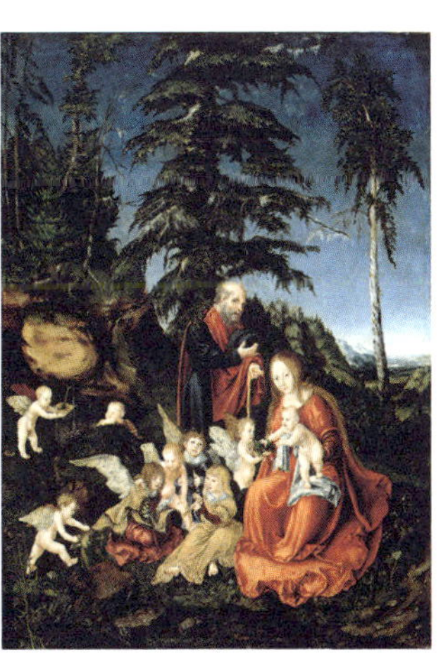

Rest on the Flight into Egypt 1504
Oil on beech wood 69 × 51 cm
Staatliche Museen zu Berlin, Gemäldegalerie

Towards the end of the fifteenth century, painters along the Danube and to the north of it adopted a style of painting which introduced the local landscape into the picture. Biblical scenes were suddenly played somewhere between Bavaria and Vienna. Dark deciduous and coniferous trees grow alongside green meadows cut through with rivers. Mist hangs over rocky mountains, and smoke rises.

For the *Rest on the Flight to Egypt*, the Holy Family must have taken a considerable detour from Bethlehem to end up in the Alps of Central Europe, where not only the fir trees grow, but a parrot acts as playmate to the angels. These first paintings that we know of from Cranach the Elder are bathed in a warm light and show an almost expressive brushstroke. Cranach traveled to the Netherlands in 1508 and was impressed by Flemish painting. Compared to the paintings of the Italian Renaissance, his colors soon become cooler, while in later years his drawing becomes more severe, his figures flatter. Something delicately bluish always shimmers under the skin of Venus. At the same time there are strong color contrasts, which make the figures look like icons; often red and orange clothes glow against a coal-black background.

The essential components of Cranach's paints are earths, resins, and minerals mixed on a glass plate in his own workshop with binding agents such as linseed oil, glue, egg-yolk, or resin.

Since Cranach had an apothecary's license, he was able to acquire pigments at trade prices. The expensive ultramarine of lapis lazuli from the Hindu Kush was available on the market in Antwerp, while yellow from the Ore Mountains could be purchased in Leipzig.

Colors that Cranach had at his disposal were, for example: lead white and vermilion red, smalt from blue cobalt glass, verdigris, Cassel earth from the German town of Kassel, and lead red, known as *mennige*. Indigo blue was made from the dried leaves of the woad plant (*Isatis tinctoria*), which in Cranach's time was grown in Thuringia, and whose flowers in bloom are not blue but yellow, like today's rape fields.

But Cranach's colors could also be called such things as: fine-marble-skin white, golden-curls red, Elbe-spray grey or bright-devil's-rust brown. And in this painting, a strawberry-reached-for-by-the-tiny-fingers-of-God-made-flesh red.

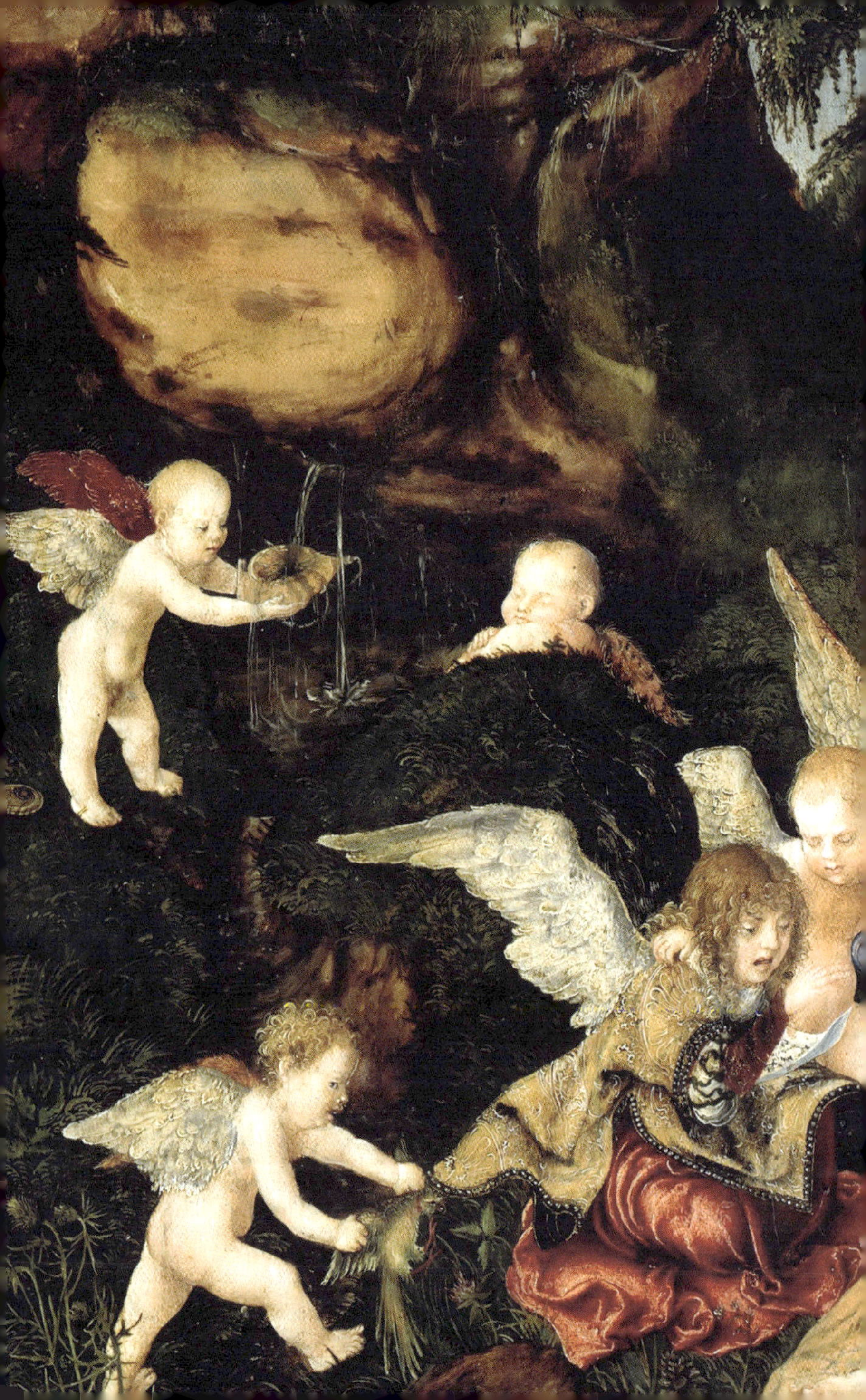

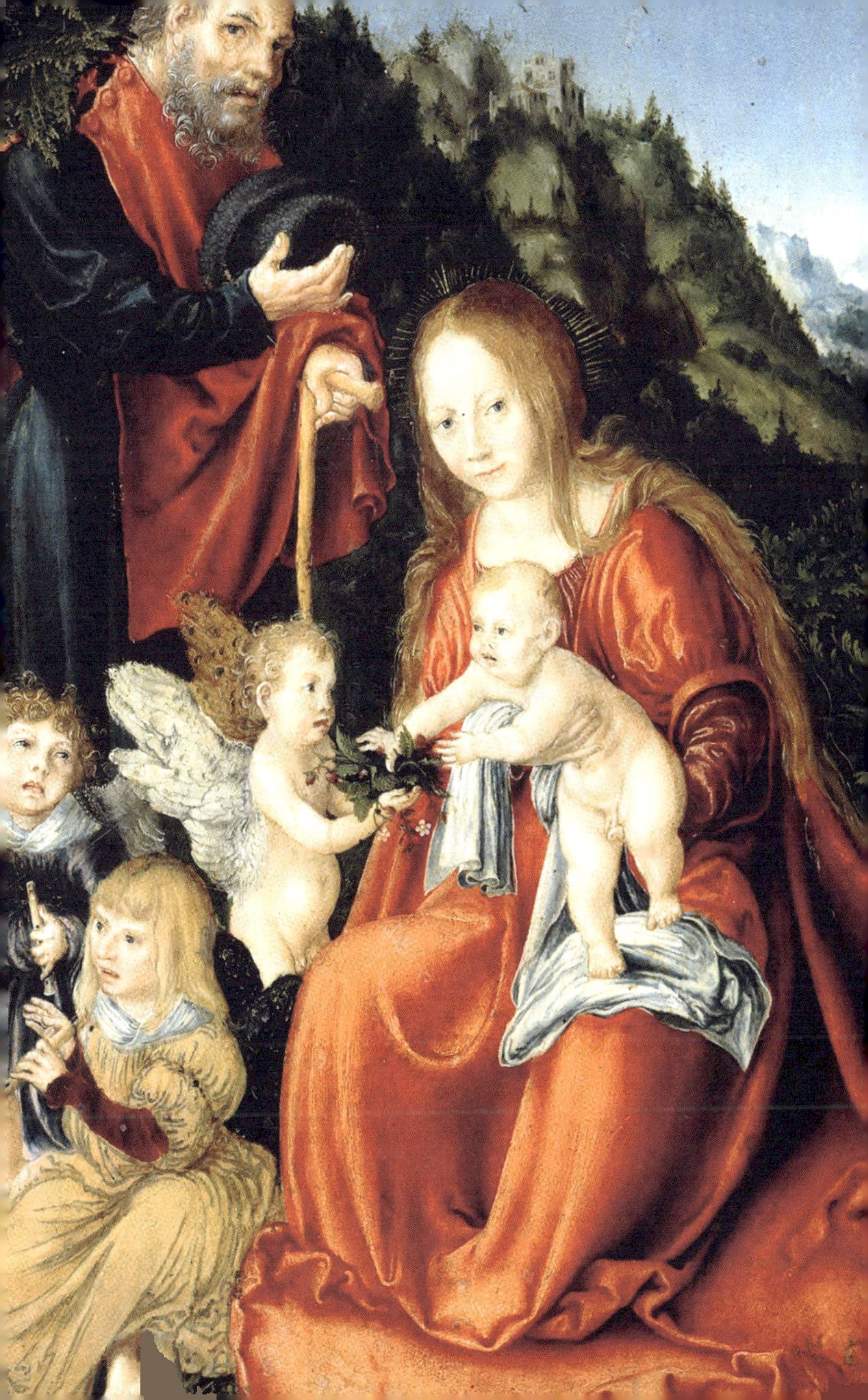

_{L →} Luther

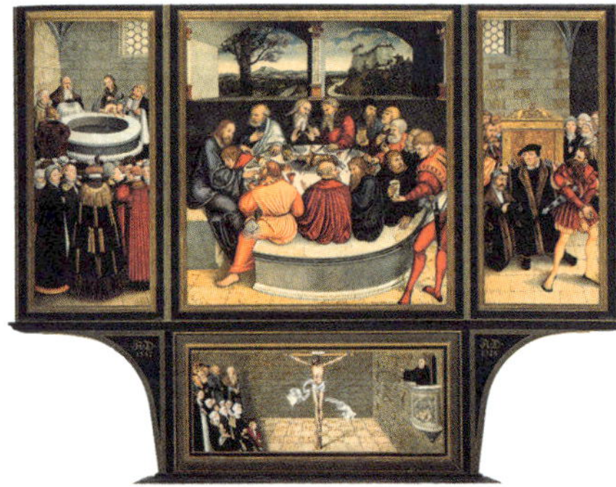

Reformation altarpiece
Stadtkirche Wittenberg 1547–1548

The Reformist Martin Luther was by no means a prince, and yet he needed something like a court painter to illustrate and disseminate his ideas. Cranach the Elder and Luther knew each other from Wittenberg, and when on October 31, 1517 the ninety-five Theses against the selling of indulgences were published and quickly spread, that set in motion a social movement of which Cranach too would become a part. In 1522, *The New Testament* in Luther's German translation, done with the help of theologians like Philipp Melanchthon, was set, illustrated, and printed in large editions in Cranach's printing workshop. Religious services were held in the German language for the first time, and the citizens of Wittenberg congregated in the city church of St. Mary. Together they elaborated themes and visual motifs to convey the new content even to those who could not read and write: Luther preached and Cranach painted.

The *Wittenberg Reformation Altarpiece* was probably conceived by Cranach the Elder and executed by Cranach the Younger and his workshop as a three-winged altarpiece. The painting on the predella, the substructure of the altar, shows an unadorned church space, Luther preaches from the pulpit, with one hand on the Bible and the other pointing towards a crucifix. On the opposite side, the congregation listens to Luther's words. We see Katharina von Bora and an elderly man with a white beard; Lucas Cranach the Elder. All gathered together

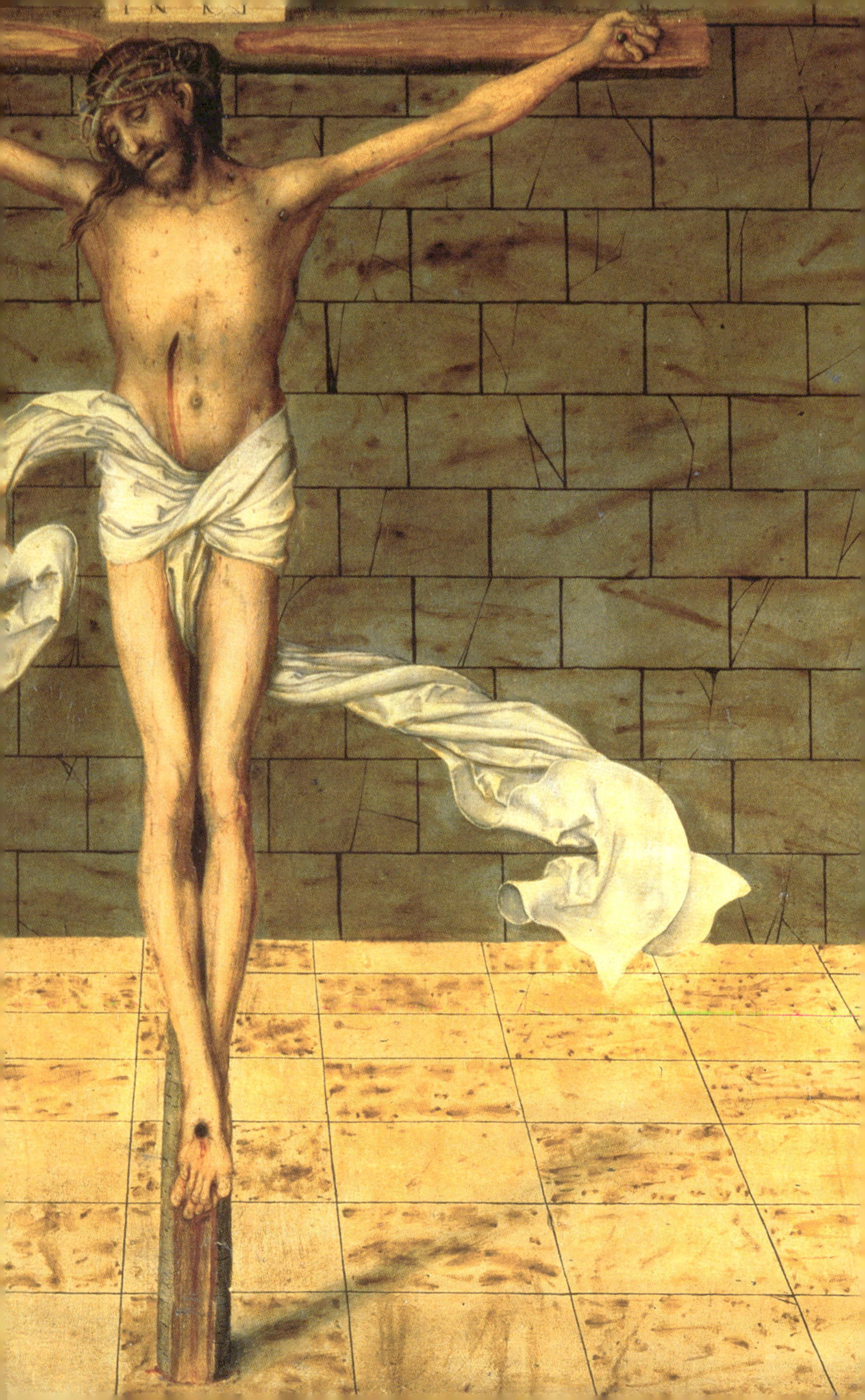

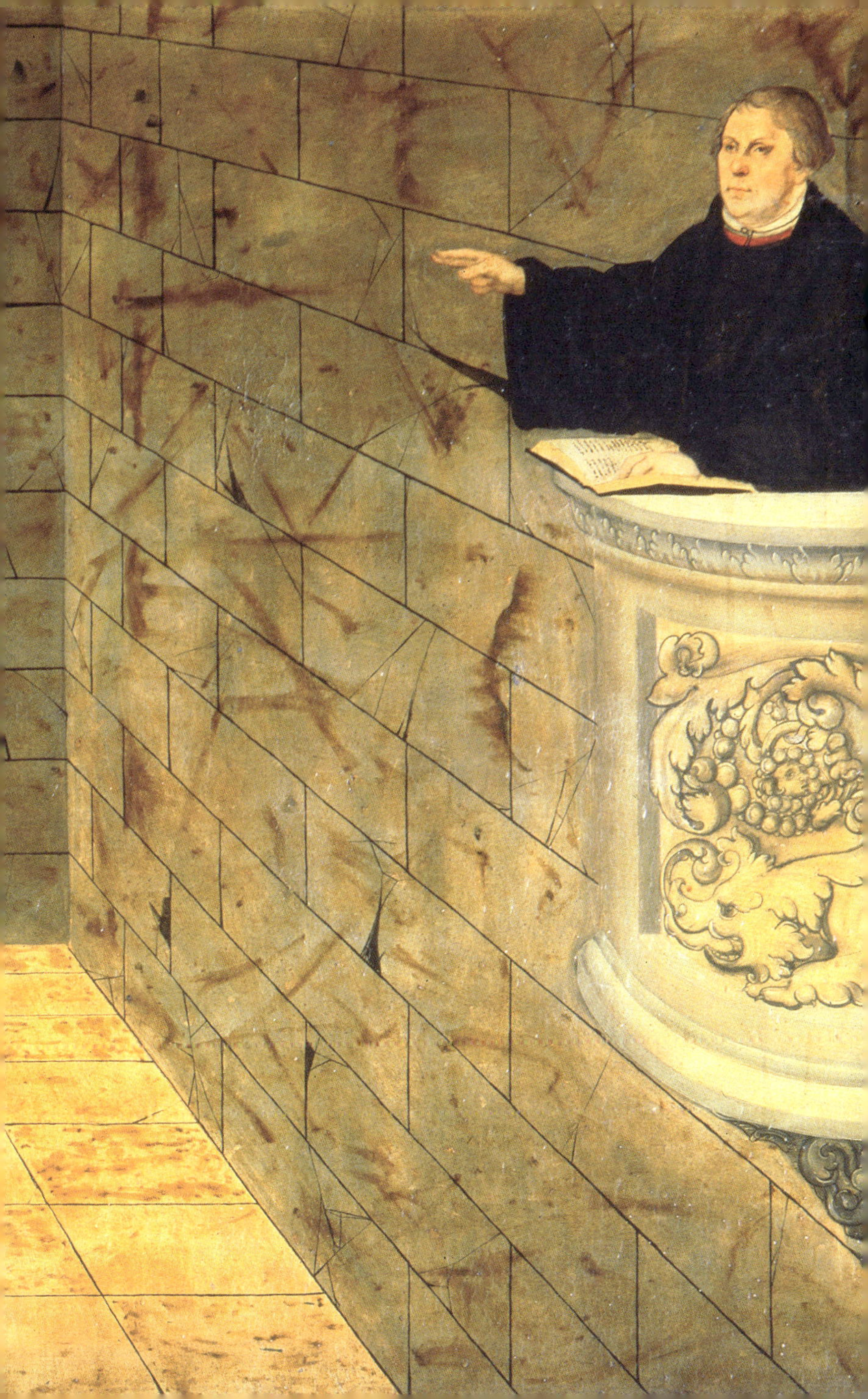

in one room, connected by looks and pointed fingers. Is Luther looking at us?

Cranach painted Luther as we imagine him even today: a young Augustinian monk with a tonsure, as "Junker Jörg," the knight with the beard working in prison in the Wartburg on his translation from the Greek, as a preacher in Wittenberg, and finally as a married burgher of the city, university professor, and reformer, well fed, with a beret and black *schaube*. And he also painted Luther on his deathbed: a bird's eye view of the deceased in a white shroud with his head laid on a pillow. Cranach is attested as having been present as a witness at Luther's wedding to the former nun Katharina von Bora. Whether Cranach and Luther were close friends we do not know, but they certainly knew each other well, Lucas and Martin from the little town of Wittenberg.

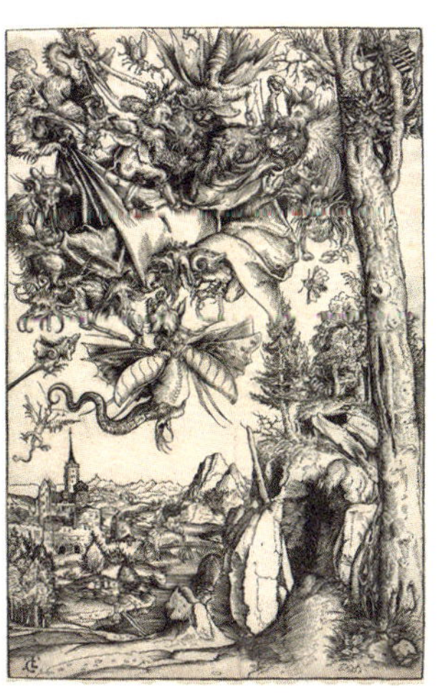

The Temptation of Saint Anthony 1509
Woodcut on paper 40.9 × 27.3 cm
Staatliche Graphische Sammlung, Munich

As well as many beautiful young men and women, Lucas Cranach also painted various monsters. These include Death and the Devil chasing after poor, sinful people, but also the caricatures and satirical images, popular and frequently copied during the Reformation, of the clergy, such as the *Papal Ass* and the *Monk's Calf*. Cranach's mischievously comical woodcuts from 1523 show scaly and furry human-animal hybrids, which Luther and Melanchthon used as illustrations to their polemical writings against the Church and Pope in Rome.

Particularly imaginative are the monsters and demons tormenting the Desert Father, St. Anthony. He gave away all his wealth and led an ascetic life. To test his faith, he went into the desert, where his spirit now had to resist temptations and his body endure all manner of torments. *The Temptation of Saint Anthony* has been a popular subject for painters since the Middle Ages, and one whose pictorial ideas are extraordinarily rich in wit and invention. Monsters at this time all look a bit alike, from the engravings of Martin Schongauer to the panels of the *Isenheim Altarpiece* by Matthias Grünewald.

In Cranach, too, St. Anthony is surrounded by a veritable mob of monsters. He is carried into the air by them, they look under his cassock, pull at his beard, they bite and pinch him. They have claws, wings, hoofs, and lizard tails,

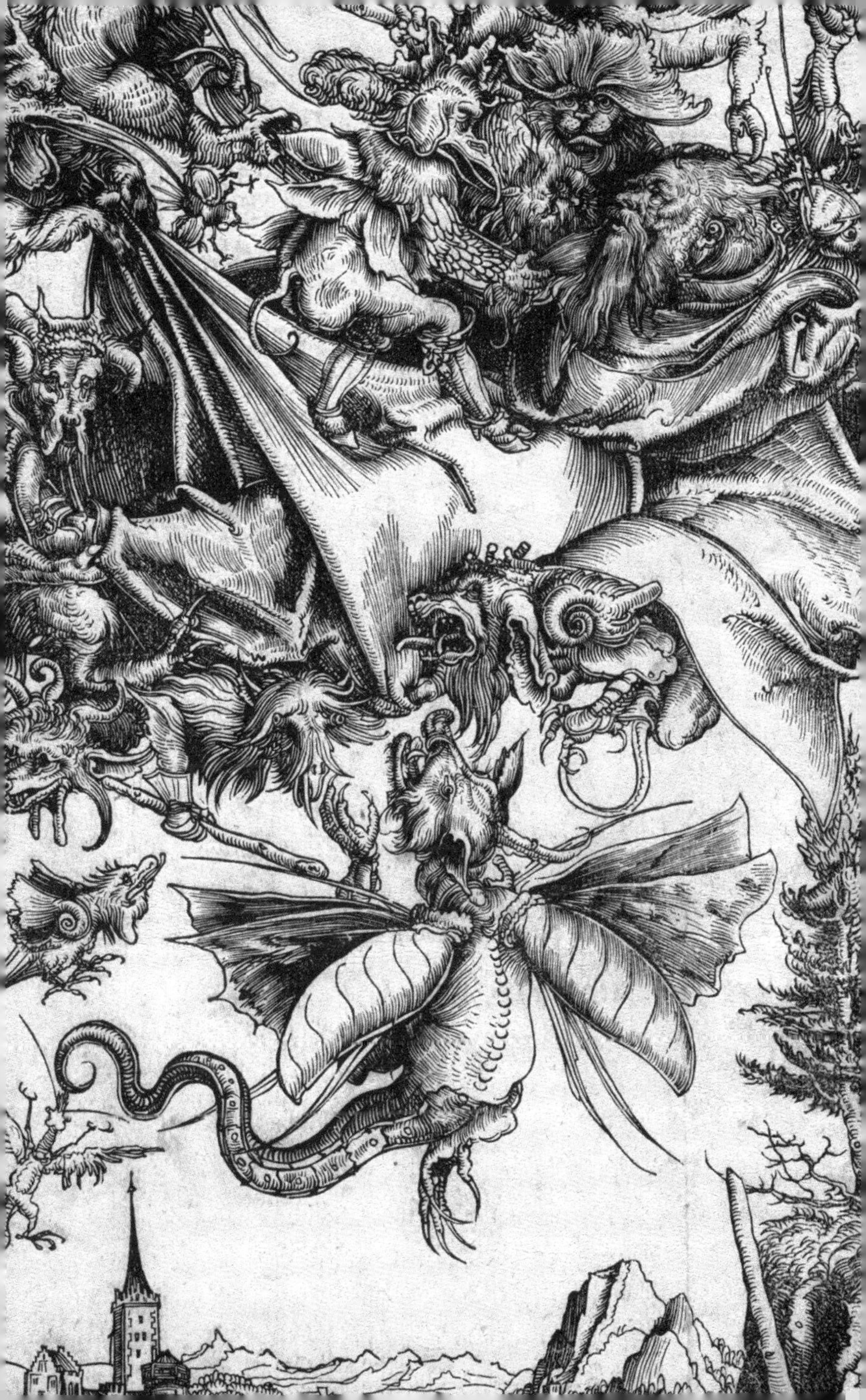

feelers, tongues, trunks, snouts, and teeth.
It's something like the picture of a nightmare
in which observation and invention have been
shaken and jumbled together in such a way that
they produce something new. What we see here
should warn us against deviating from the right
path, but we can't tear our eyes away from the
spectacle. This delight in fear that we feel
at the sight of horror—it is the offspring of all
of art's monsters.

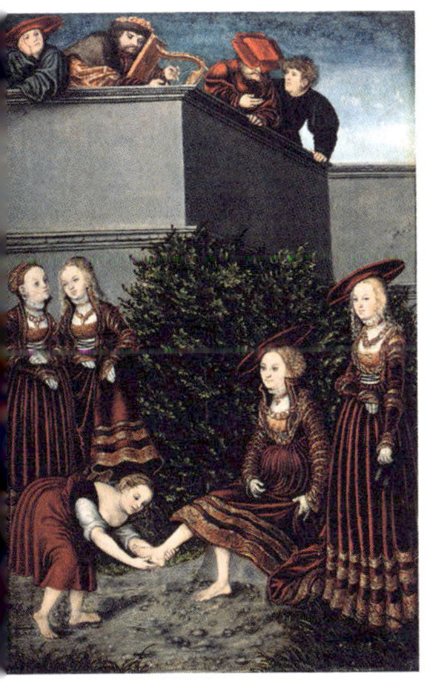

David and Bathsheba 1526
Mixed media on beech wood 36 × 24 cm
Staatliche Museen zu Berlin, Gemäldegalerie

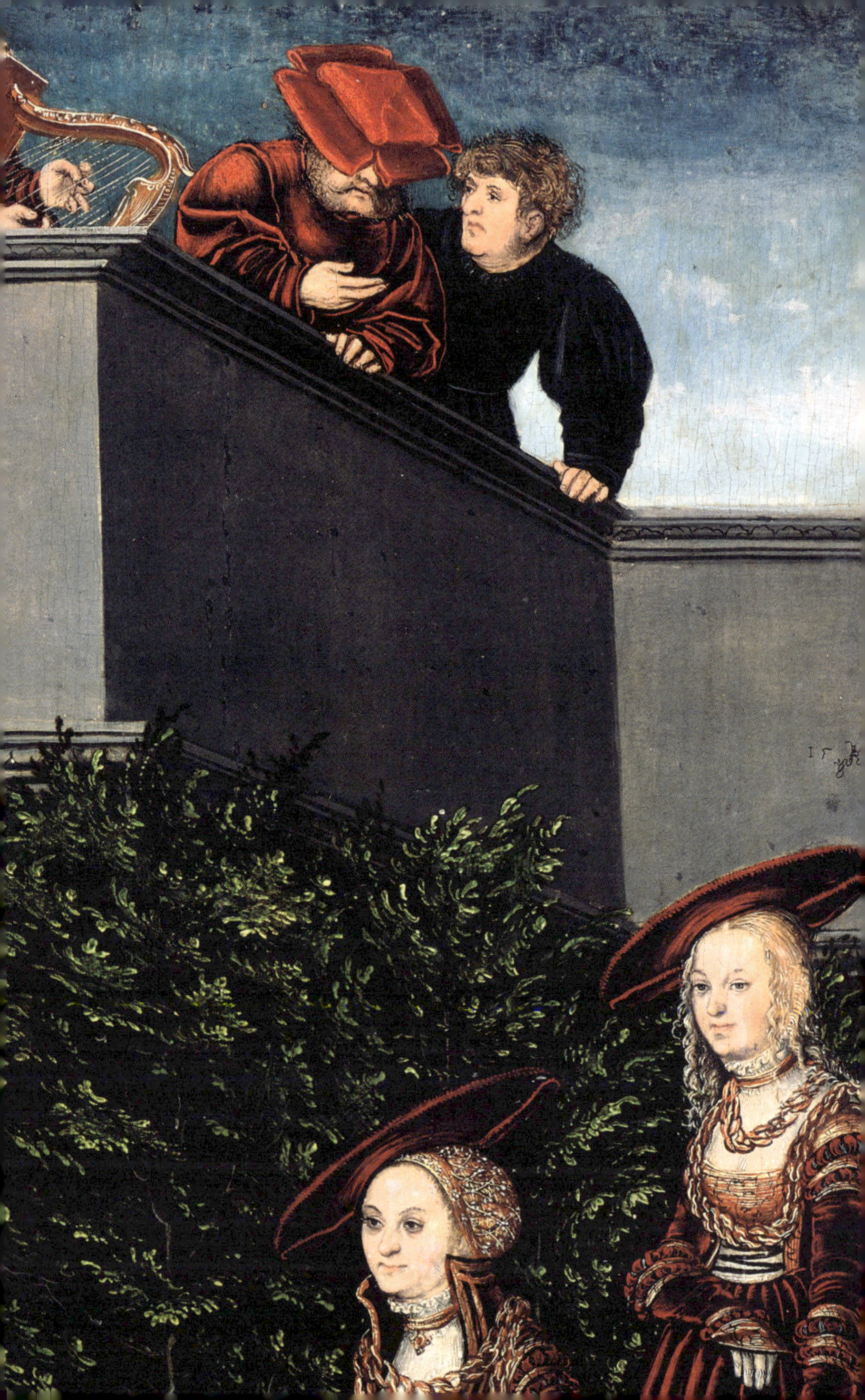

Cranach's paintings call for many leading roles: Lot and his daughters, Judith and Holofernes, Christ and the woman taken in adultery, Venus and Cupid, Dr. Cuspinian and the wife of Dr. Cuspinian, Martin Luther and Katharina von Bora. And there are David and Bathsheba: King David observes Bathsheba in the bath and wants to have her for himself, even though she is another man's wife. David takes up his harp and plays for Bathsheba, having already elaborated his plans to murder her husband.

The painting *David and Bathsheba* shows a scene that Cranach painted and reinvented many times. Strikingly, it is the smooth grey wall that divides the story in two. It divides the two protagonists from one another and looks as if it has been collaged onto the picture. David has three companions at the top of the wall with him, who have a good view of the women in the bath down below, but the three are entirely preoccupied with themselves: the first may be dreaming of someone else, the last quizzically observes David as he plays his music, and the companion in the middle looks as if he is staring with fascination at a smartphone in his right hand. His red hat with a brim is painted so clumsily that it looks as if it's flapping flatly downwards. It sits like a foreign body over his half-covered face and turns this minor player into one of the strangest figures in Cranach's paintings.

The many extras in the background of a painting play minor roles, as in *The Death of Holofernes* where they form a circle with the saddled horses in the middle. A swarm of heads also appears in Ascension scenes: disembodied angels' heads fly through a strip of cloud. God, whom we are reluctant to call a bit-part actor, flies as a loose, white-bearded head across the sky, sending yellow rays to the earth. And we might mention one in particular among these wonderfully skewed bit-parts: in the representation of *Law and Grace (Law and the Gospel)*, painted around 1535, Jesus' legs fly towards a yellow sky. Grace could not look more cheerful!

0 → Ornament

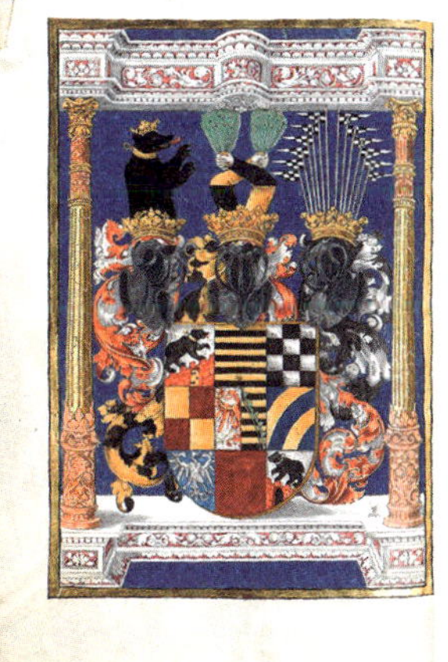

Lucas Cranach the Younger (Workshop)
Coat of arms of Anhalt from the Cranach Bible 1941
Anhaltische Landesbücherei Dessau

From the beginning of the sixteenth century clothes were slit to improve freedom of movement for elbows, knees, and thighs. The colorful lining beneath was revealed, and in its painterly reproduction it shows a strict pattern that sometimes moves through the entire painting. Often the figures thus ornamented stand against a monochrome blue, grey, green, black, orange, or yellow background.

Hair, jewelry, and clothes form color contrasts, often between black, white, and red. The symmetry in the configuration of the figures reinforces the impression of the ornamental. This is joined in landscape paintings and group or crowd scenes by Cranach's evident delight in the representation and elaboration of detail and an almost painstaking painterly inventory of all participants.

Colorful coats of arms with minute patterns are often an integral component of portraits, and even today they help us to identify the individuals depicted. It was also one of the tasks of a court painter to design these coats of arms.

Cranach is a painter of surfaces, his application of paint is economical and transparent, with little impasto. He paints both princesses and burghers in the fashionable clothes of the day, the men in armor or festively dressed—sometimes with a codpiece worn over the middle of the hose for emphasis—or in the garb of humanist

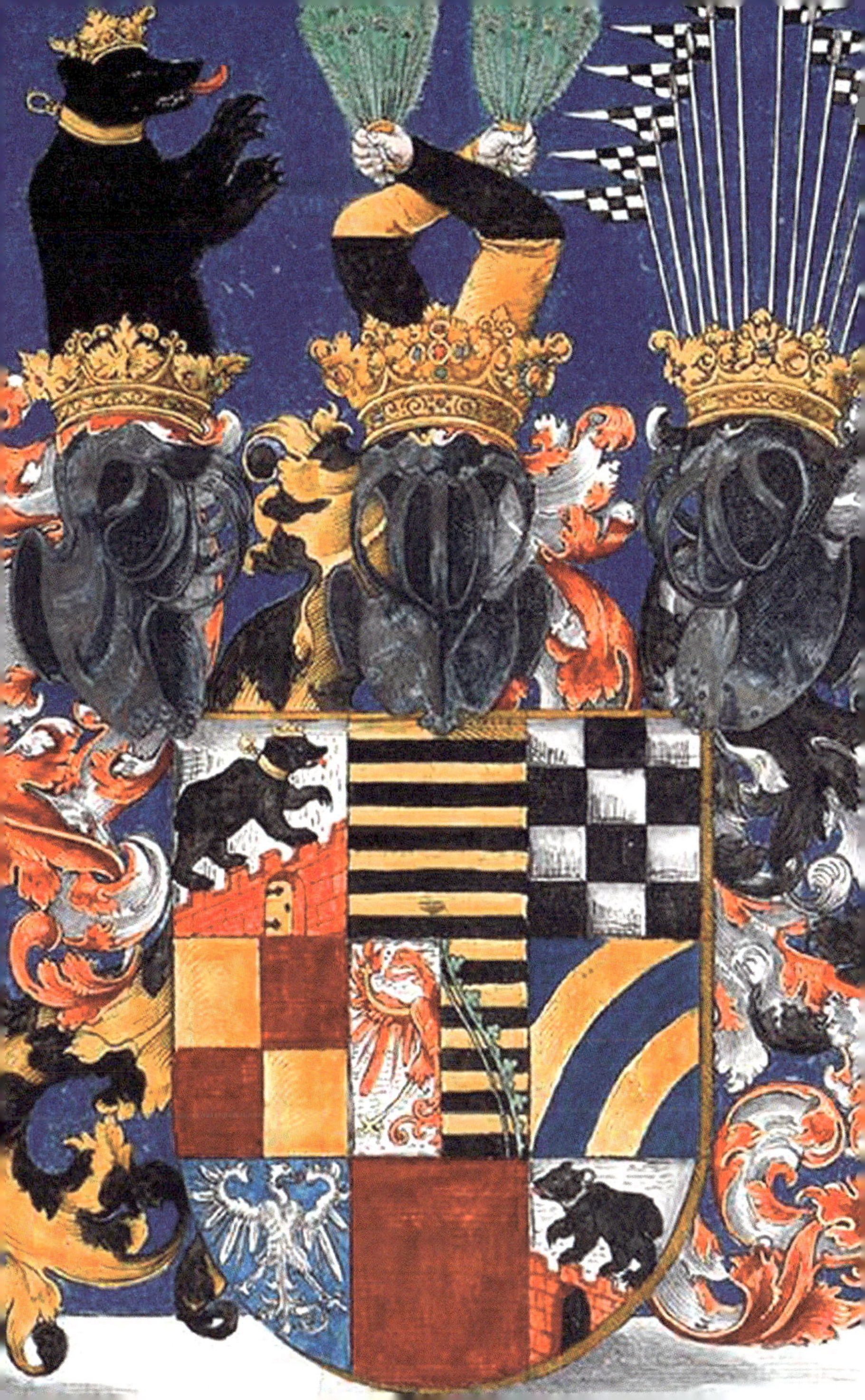

scholars with *schaube* and beret. Over their shirts they wear a tight doublet with a round neck or a stiff collar tied at the front.

The comical aspect of Cranach's paintings for present-day viewers arises from the fact that that ornamentation has lost its significance: the hierarchies of the time, both of the church and the nobility, no longer apply. For that reason, we may be struck all more clearly by the stiffness of the poses and posture. Those status symbols are now without influence and power, those accessories and ornaments are now replaced by new forms of representation.

But perhaps precisely that is the invitation to perceive in Cranach's painting first and foremost the formal language of paint and brush, and only on a second examination to read into them the very different stories that lie beneath.

P → Picasso

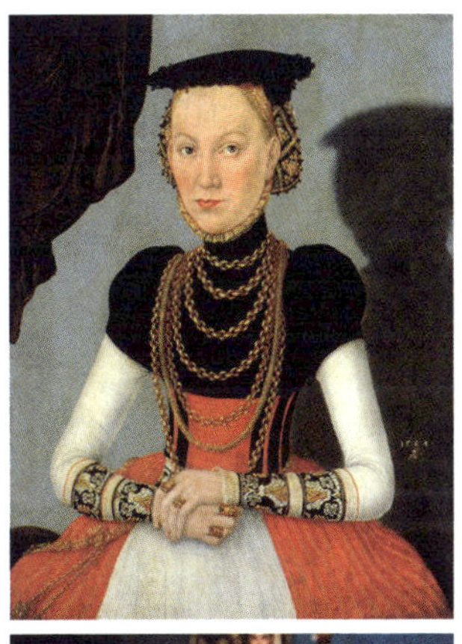

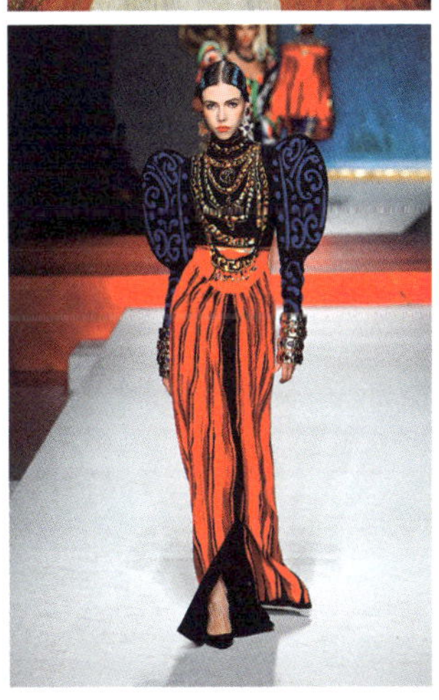

Lucas Cranach the Younger
Portrait of a Young Woman 1564
Lime wood 83.5 × 63.7 cm
Kunsthistorisches Museum Vienna,
Picture Gallery

Jeremy Scott for Moschino
Spring/Summer 2020
after Pablo Picasso *Portrait de jeune fille,
d'après Cranach le Jeune* 1958

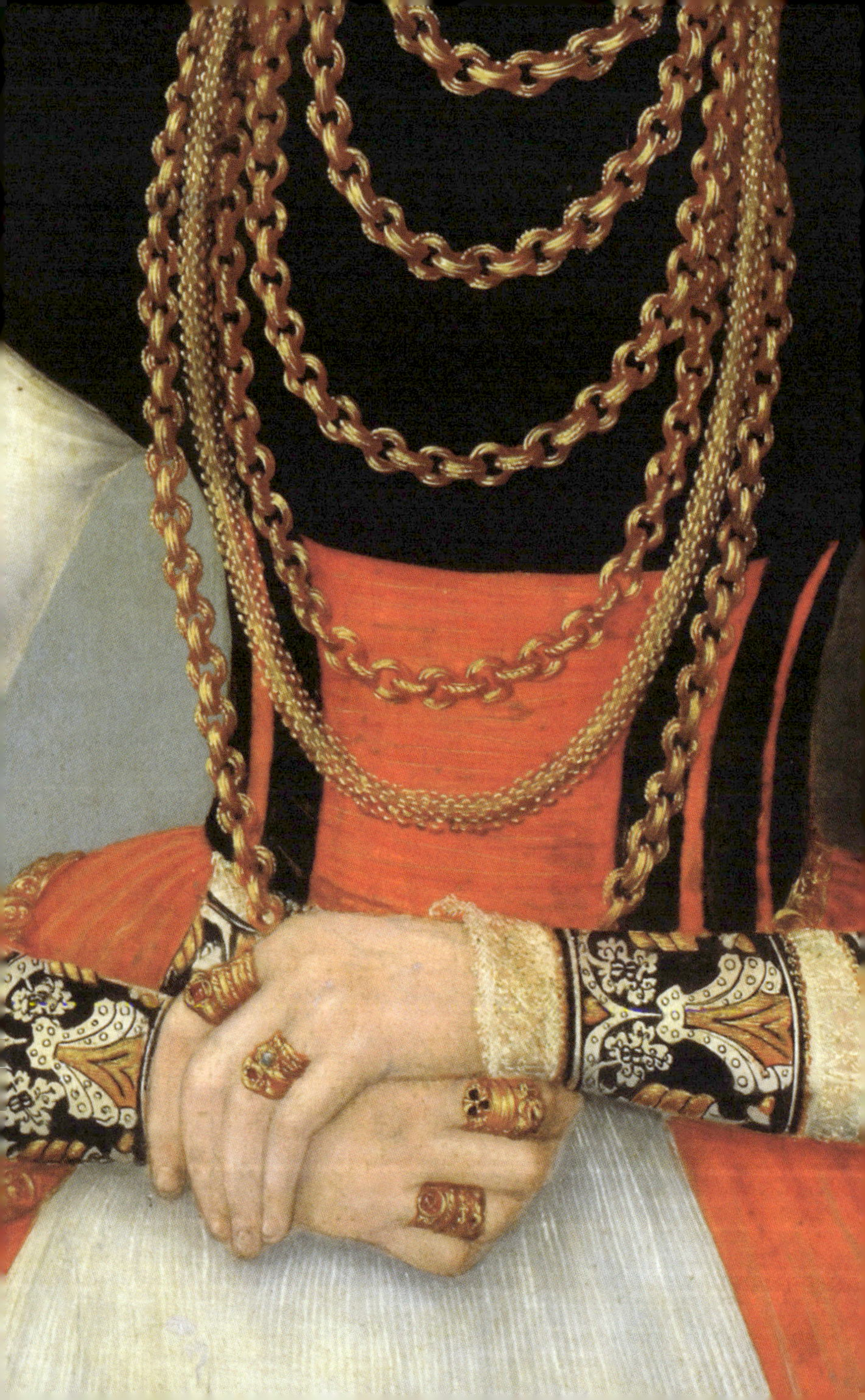

According to legend, Pablo Picasso once received a postcard from Vienna sent by his art dealer and friend Daniel-Henry Kahnweiler. It shows the wonderful 1564 *Portrait of a Young Woman* by Lucas Cranach the Younger. In 1958, Picasso made a linocut of his interpretation of the painting, the *Portrait de jeune fille, d'après Cranach le Jeune*. In this "elimination print" all six colors were printed with a single plate of linoleum, which was reworked with the gouge after each application of paint. Picasso's paraphrase looks like its model, except that the young woman's face has more cubist oddity about it than the original, and the white sleeves have now been dyed blue.

And then comes the most powerful intervention: for the print the lino plate is painted with a roller, a sheet of paper is placed on the plate and both go to the printing press. When the finished sheet is then pulled away, the picture appears on the paper: as a reverse image. And that's also what happened to Picasso, who was hardly unsettled by such trivia.

There is also a pendant to the *Portrait of a Young Woman—Male Portrait*. It is, seen from the picture's-eye-view, supposed to be to the right of the wife, exactly the spot where a male portrait had "heraldically" to be placed at this time. In Picasso's reflection, the female pendant assumes the leading role in this double portrait, even though it's not what the artist intended.

Where Picasso drew his inspiration from Cranach, the fashion label Moschino, with its designer Jeremy Scott, in turn drew inspiration from Picasso. In the 2020 Spring/Summer collection the *Portrait de jeune fille, d'après Cranach le Jeune* was brought to life and walked with thick gold bracelets down the catwalk, the dress printed with the gold chains that once belonged to the sixteenth century.

Even today Cranach inspires artists to respond to his work. We find interpretations by artists such as Otto Dix, Ernst Ludwig Kirchner, Alberto Giacometti, Fernando Botero, Andy Warhol, and Yasumasa Morimura. In its 2020–2021 exhibition *Cranach: Artist and Innovator*, Compton Verney in the UK, showed paintings by John Currin, the minutely detailed landscape paintings of the Indian painter Raqip Shaw, and a ceramic Venus with a red sun visor by Claire Partington along-side works by Cranach. There is a dance piece by William Forsythe with Cranach in the title and the now-famous intro to the American television series *Desperate Housewives* with the animated curls of a Cranach Eve. So stylish!

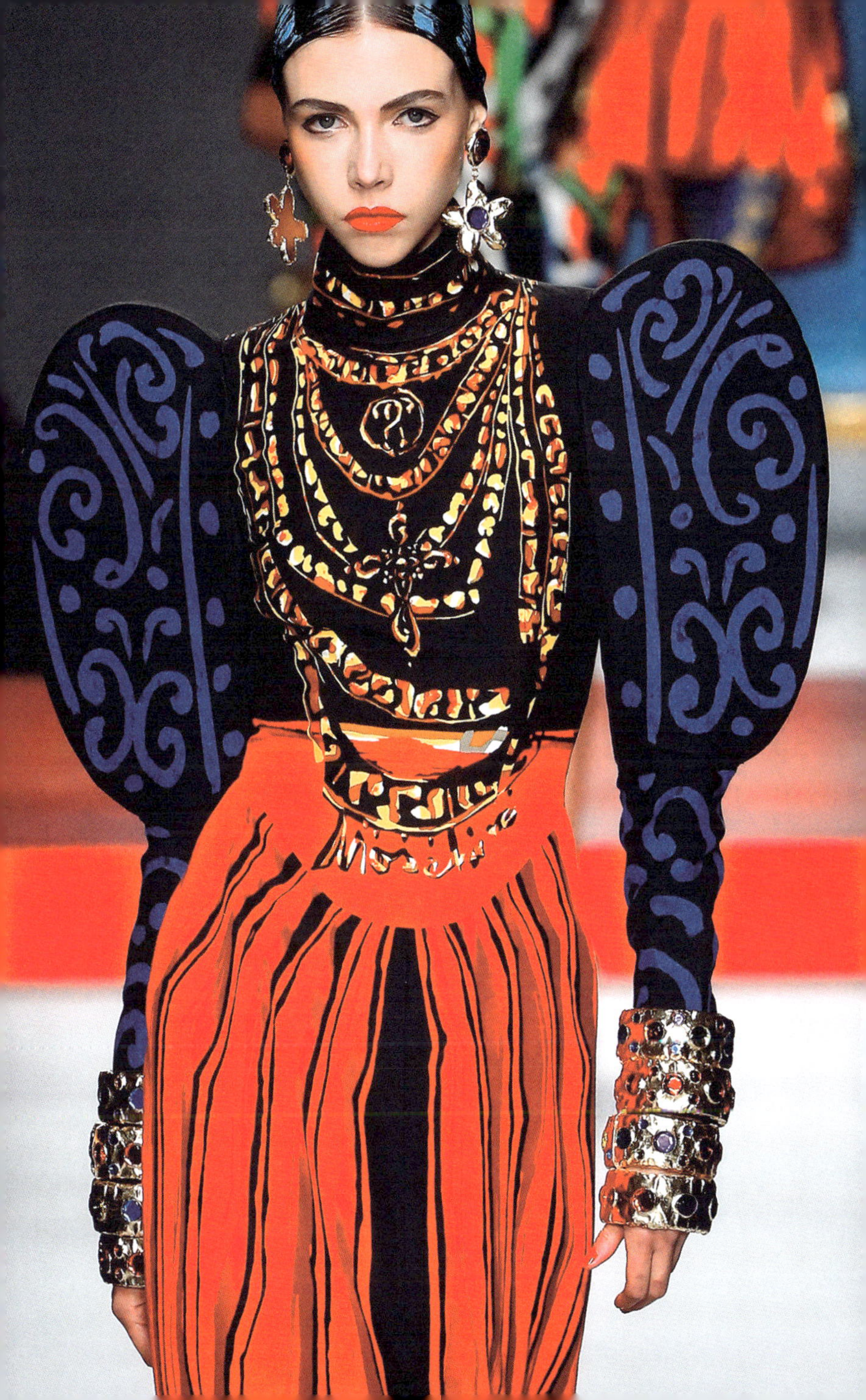

Receipt from Cranach's workshop:
Cranach receives cost of an invoice for gold leaf,
silver and chimney soot reimbursed 1509

Even in those days paintings were luxury goods. A small painted panel from the workshop of Cranach, who was famous even in his own life-time, cost 4 guilders, the annual income of a domestic servant. With his appointment as court painter, Cranach the Elder received an annual income of 100 guilders, comparable to the income of a university professor at the time. In addition, he received reimbursements for painting materials and travel expenses. The profits from his wine shop made between 500 and 900 guilders a year, and there was also an apothecary shop, and seven or eight properties. These were later joined by the print works, which printed the Luther Bible in large editions. Cranach soon became one of the wealthiest burghers in Wittenberg.

A piece of paper documents the transition from the natural economy to the money economy, which had already occurred at this time. Cranach's workshop kept such thorough accounts of income and expenditure that the correspondence is still comprehensible even 500 years later. As if in a diary, we can read how Cranach's daily life was constituted: one day he is a lay judge at court, on another day he is paying a messenger or buying winter clothes for his assistants.

We find paper documents, written with pen and Indian ink: about taxes paid and payments received for painted canvases, the design of a Bible, for the coloring of figures, the gilding of letters, for binding with velvet and frames.

A handwritten receipt from 1509 records how the painter received the costs for a bill concerning gold leaf, silver, and soot: "*Lucas malern zugeschickt*" ("Sent to painter Lucas"). Paid by the donor Frederick the Wise on request: 8 guilders for 2 quires gold, 1 guilder and 3 groschen for 2 quires of silver. (A quire is an old measurement for paper; in the trade in gold leaf and silver it amounts to around 12–25 sheets.) Also listed: 1 guilder and 15 groschen for 1 quire *Zwischgold* (gold leaf layered with silver on the reverse); and 1 guilder, 8 groschen, 8 denars for 40 cans of *Kadlofram* (soot from the chimney. One "can," according to region, came to around a liter).

Incidentally, a contemporary of Cranach's, the master scribe Johann Neudörffer from Nuremberg, was involved in the development of gothic and German cursive scripts: German script emerges from gothic cursive, which is written fluently by hand, linking the individual letters together. Today, the receipt from Cranach's workshop looks like an elegantly curved calligraphic poem.

guld dem gleußman zu Aldenburg zalt
hat er den barfußer monch daselbst
vf beuelh geben

guld Botharty einem knecht der bey kurch
zabil wundt wird in der aufrulz herrisch
Schenck Otten vnd tem hansen von minckwicz

guld vf beuelh pfeffinger Lorenczn
goltschmidt zu Torgau geben Mitwoch Ciriaci

guld fur ij buch fein golt
guld ingt fur ij buch alb   Lucas malern
guld er gt fur j buch franntsch golt   zugesthickt
guld vm gt viij d fur gol. ten kadloßram   .

guld vij schilling golt vf beuelh pfeffingers
Andresen matzer zu leipzk zalt fur
etlich stempfel zu Augspurg vnd vogel
die vogel hmt von Jnnßbruck gen Nu
inberg an die solckmatin gesthickt

guld vf beuelh pfeffinger tem Sebastian
hennioch fur sein presencz weil er vf der
rechnung zu Torgau gewest vij wochn

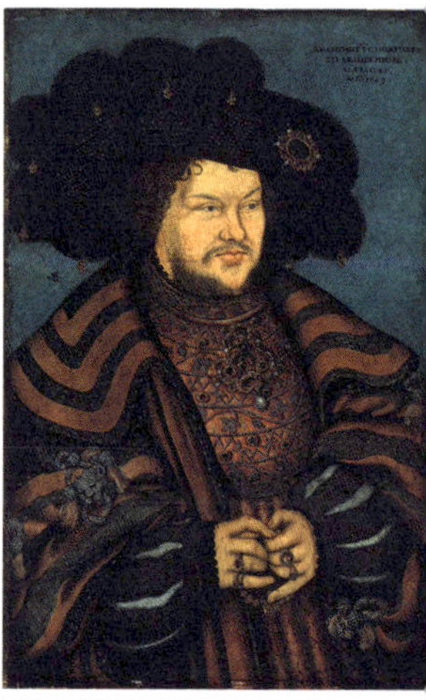

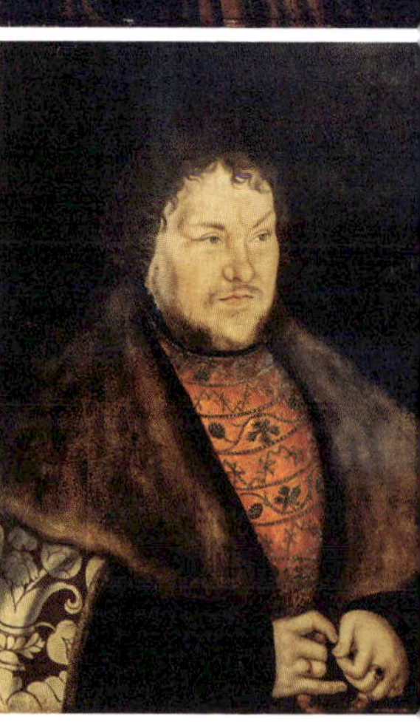

*Portrait of the Joachim I Nestor
Elector of Brandenburg* 1529
Oil on beech wood 63.7 × 42.2 cm
Bayerische Staatsgemäldesammlungen,
Staatsgalerie Aschaffenburg,
Johannisburg Castle

*Portrait of the Joachim I Nestor
Elector of Brandenburg* 1529
Oil on wood 52 × 35.5 cm
Stiftung Preußische Schlösser und Gärten,
Potsdam

Cranach's paintings are testament to originality, a wealth of invention, beauty, and wit. To paint like Cranach, it does not take a trick or ruse—it takes skill, subtlety, curiosity, and a delight in composition. However, in order to paint like that and produce thousands of paintings, Cranach required a technique that simplified production and shortened the process. Cranach's special trick—the technique that turned him into the "fastest" painter, as it says on his gravestone in Weimar (Cranach the Elder died in 1553)—allowed him to delegate the individual steps to colleagues, while still preserving a unified style. (Whether it was actually the "fastest," *celerrimus*, that was meant and not perhaps the "most celebrated," *celeberrimus*, is a matter for speculation.) Albrecht Dürer, for example, also had a workshop but no standardized painting style. The work process was divided up, from grounding and preparatory drawing to painting and varnishing.

The individual subjects were assembled from templates. The preliminary study for the portrait was presumably drawn by the artist in the immediate presence of the model, and later stored in the workshop, along with other common motifs. This provides the face of the sitter as a model, after which any kind of clothing can be placed on them, or signs of ageing added later. In the tracing process the outlines of the drawn model are copied with red chalk or charcoal dust and wooden sticks on paper, and thus transferred to a new ground. The picture

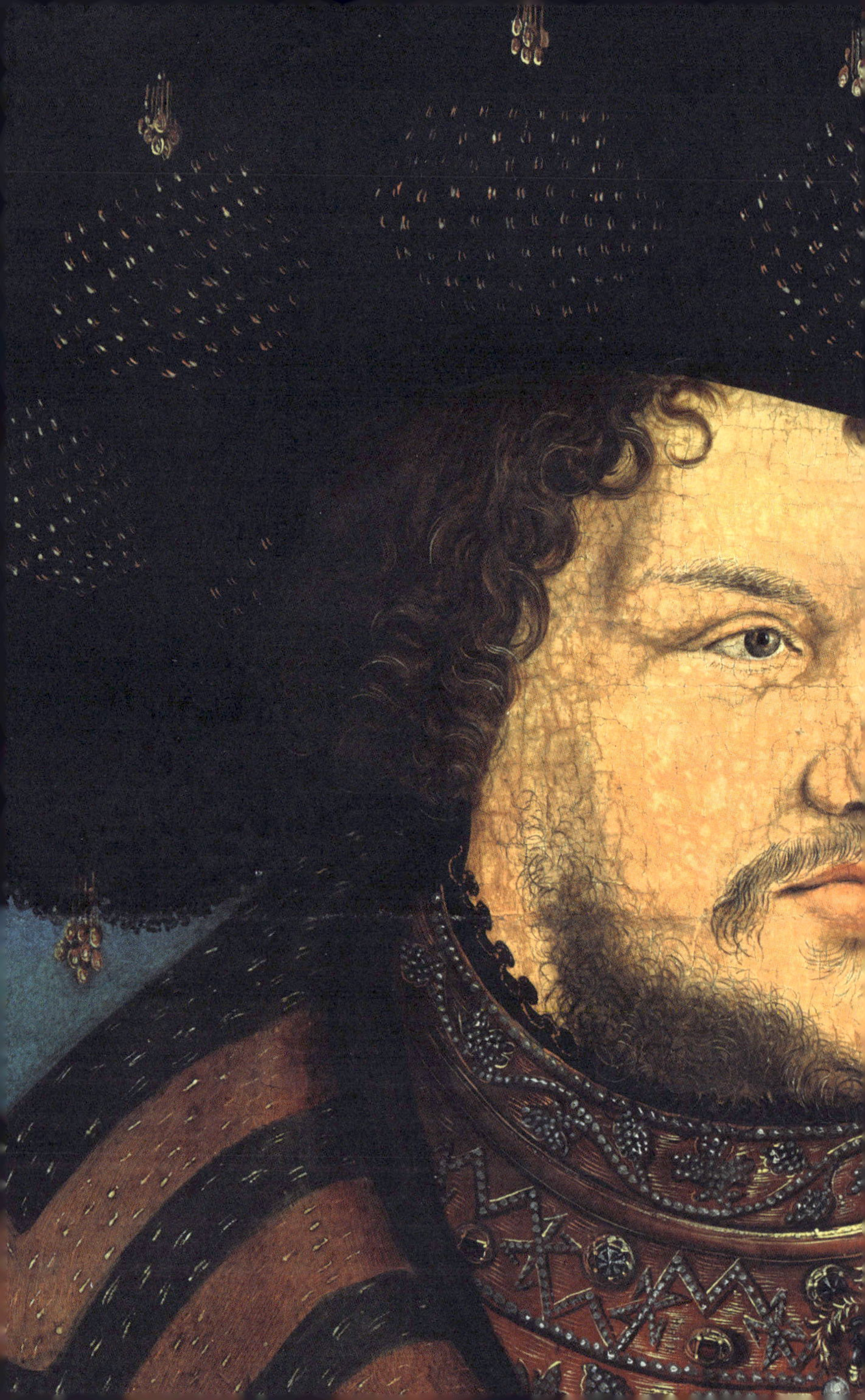

supports, often wooden panels, had fixed formats and were cut to size.

Thus, what is revealed to today's eyes is not necessarily the celebration of the individual painting, but a celebration of the serial. Cranach's paintings are highly recognizable, the sitters appear stylized, perhaps also a little detached and stiff, as if they were figures from a fairy tale. Then again, we also find very naturalistic features, particularly in male portrait subjects.

Yes, a tendency towards the schematic was certainly cultivated in the Cranach workshop, and it can also exert an incredible charm upon the viewer.

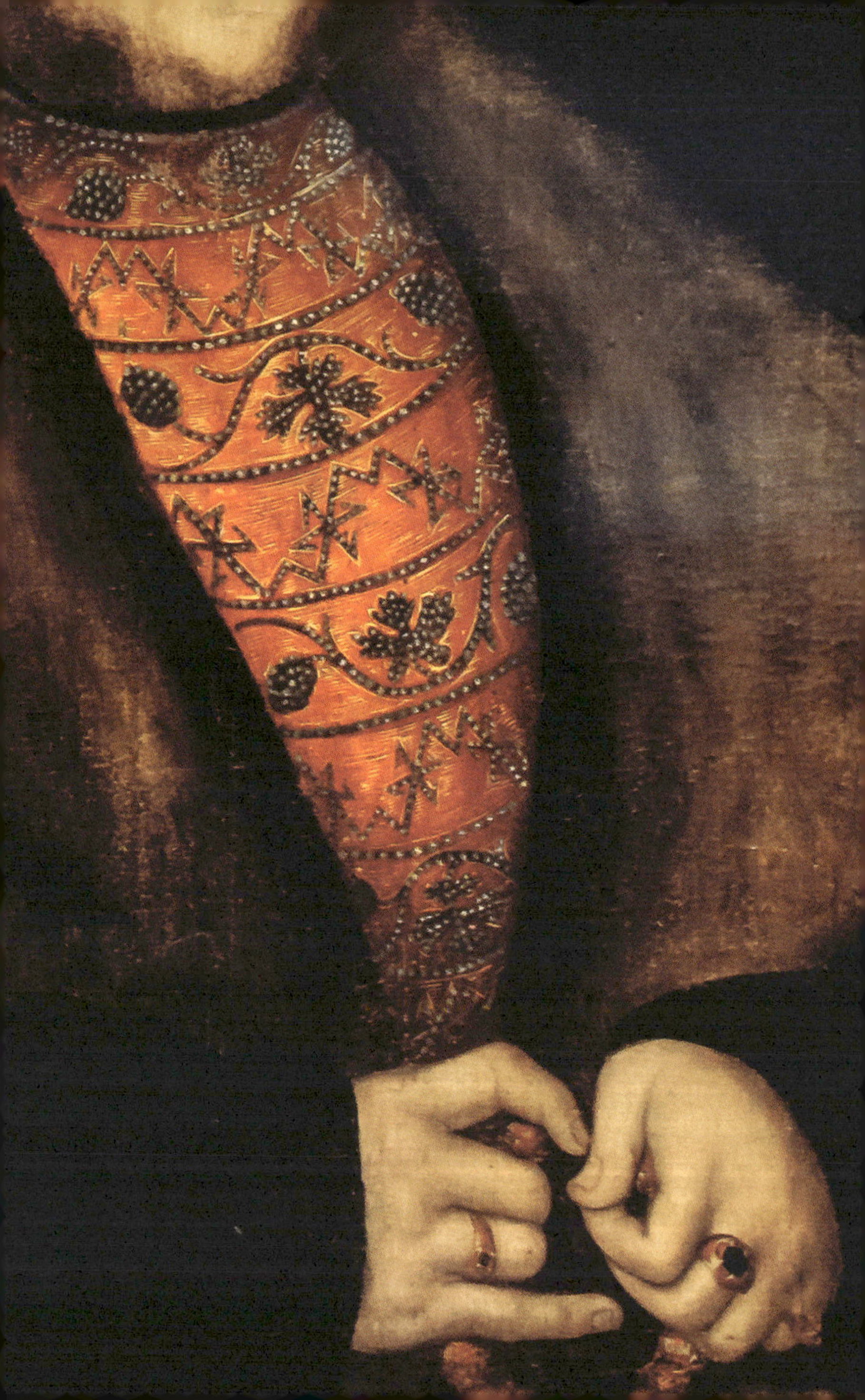

s→ Scrapbook

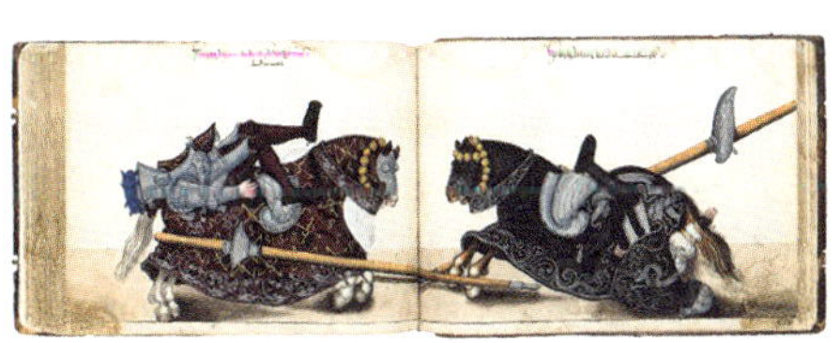

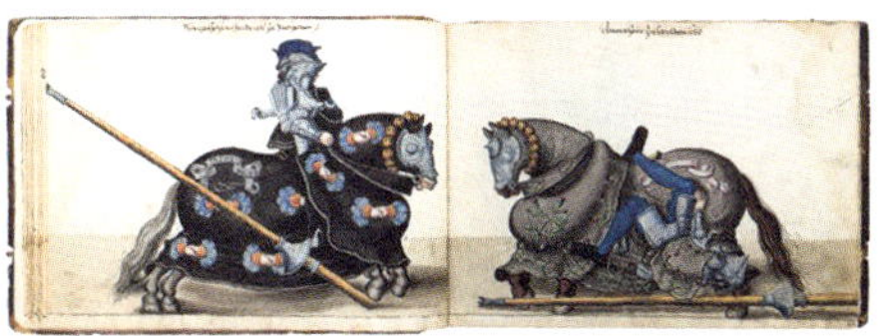

Lucas Cranach the Elder, workshop
*Tournament book of Duke John Frederick
the Magnanimous of Saxony* ca. 1540
Art Collection of the Veste Coburg

For as long as people have hunted, they have also gathered. Today this passion for collection is readily apparent among children, with their colorful stickers of footballers or superhero characters, which they eagerly exchange with one another before sticking them in a scrapbook.

As a painter, Cranach was also a collector, not least because of his clients' wishes. The Elector of Saxony, John Frederick the Magnanimous, once ordered over sixty portraits of a gallery of ancestors from him. The sheer quantity of such a portrait offensive serves as a demonstration of power—one places oneself into a community of many—and a consolidation of it. At the same time, the collection, the series, or list has the character of documentation at a time when there were neither photographs nor newspapers to commemorate or report upon events. In the *Tournament Book of Duke John Frederick the Magnanimous*—Cranach's third court client from 1532 onwards—the Cranach workshop produced a kind of scrapbook.

The tournament book, now on display in Veste Coburg (Coburg Fortress) in Germany, is small enough to hold in one's hand to leaf through its many pages, which show—in numerous variations—the knight on his tournament horse, carrying lances blunt and sharp, with armor for protection and the visor of his helmet closed. Double page spreads show an artistically repre- sented confrontation between two opponents,

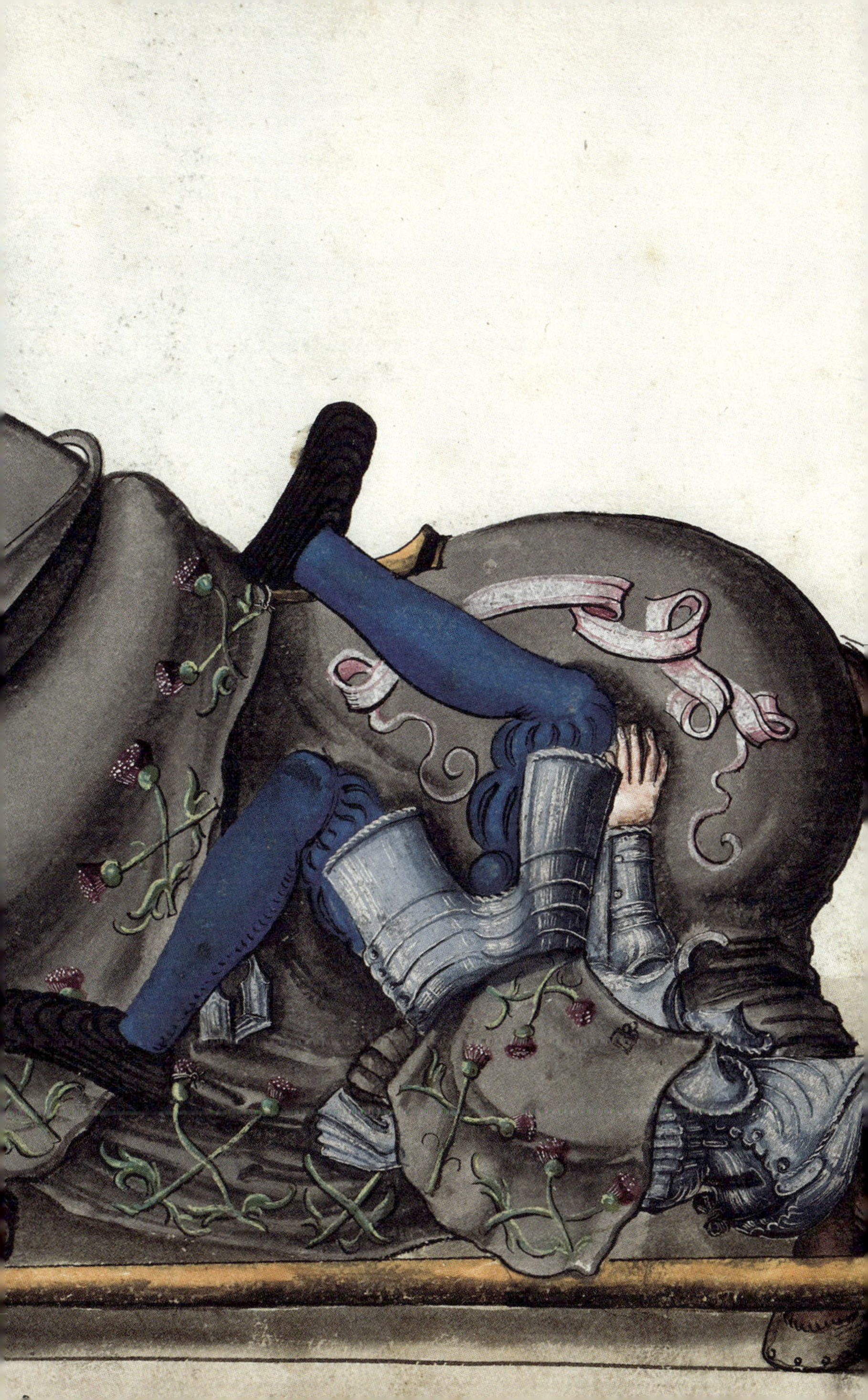

either sitting firmly in the saddle or falling from their horses in the most entertaining contortions. Not least, these paintings also document the chivalric fashions of the time, as well as recording another task of the court painter: the design of the caparisons, banners, and festive decorations. Tournaments were held to coincide with weddings and festivals, and it was Cranach's task to be present, observe the event, make sketches, and later produce woodcuts and paintings of the proceedings.

The fact that the colors have been so powerfully preserved makes the tournament book a particular pleasure. Andy Warhol's drawings of shoes and cats are hardly more colorful—they are a modern example of the artistic principle of the series.

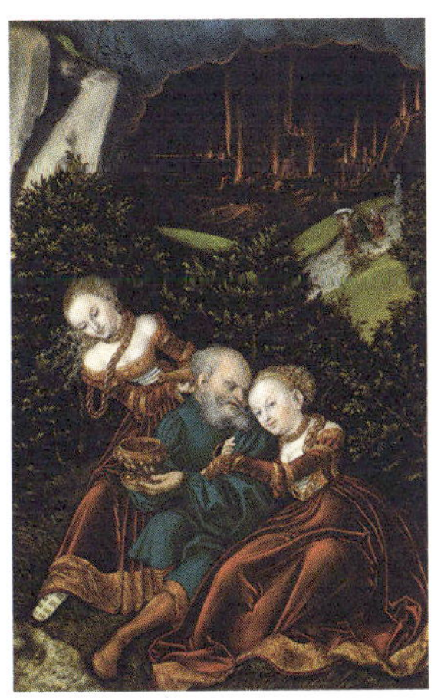

Lot and his Daughters 1528
Beech wood 56 × 37 cm
Kunsthistorisches Museum Vienna,
Picture Gallery

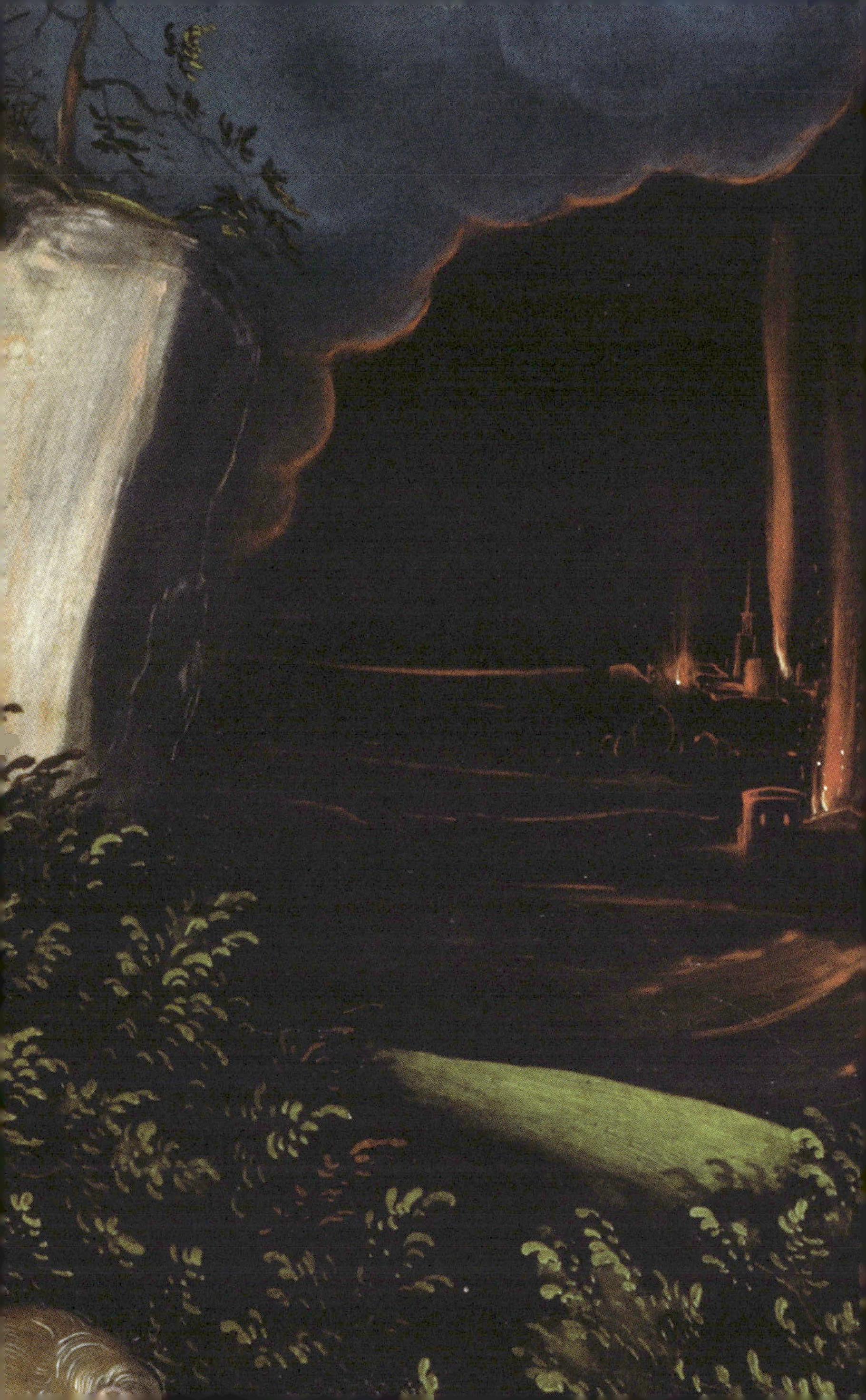

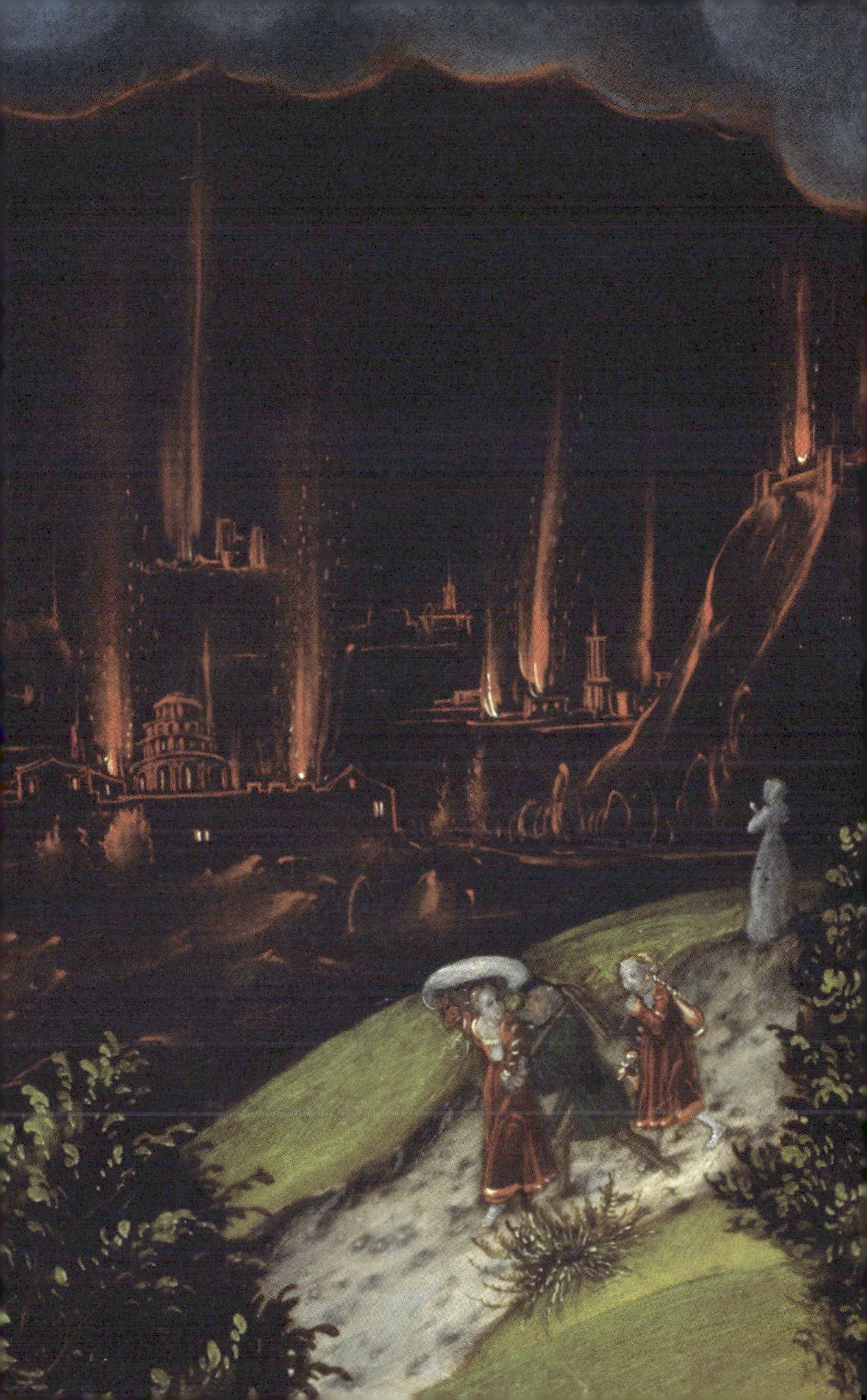

Doom threatens in the distance, in the background. It is not orderly like the ornament of the Golden Age and Paradise, wherever two and two lie together, embrace, bathe, snack on grapes. Doom is a flaming inferno, flickering and red, into which sinful humans run, fleeing Death and the Devil, as in the 1529 painting *Law and Grace (Law and the Gospel)*.

It may be something like a personal doom that rushes towards one through the melancholy that gives the allegorical painting of 1532 its title. In *Melancholy*, a little child sits swinging on a rope. Doom hovers in the form of clouds accompanied as in a nightmare by dark figures, a fierce boar ridden by an emaciated human, clutching a strap with which he holds another prisoner.

Cranach often uses clouds, weather, and lowering skies as forebodings and premonitions, but also as warning of impending calamity. While looking at the painting, we ourselves still have the possibility of turning the corner in our own lives.

So, while we may be wary of adversity, the painter seems to have taken pure delight in its elaboration. The end of the world depicted in the fall of Sodom looks crazily psychedelic in the background of the three figures from the painting *Lot and His Daughters*. The true disaster in this story from the Old Testament is played out among the peaceful-looking trio in the foreground. First Lot "offered" his virgin daughters to the raging mob, but then the city of Sodom was destroyed leaving Lot and his daughters alive. A second version of the biblical story, which we can also read as a kind of perpetrator-victim reversal, tells that the daughters get their father drunk in order to seduce him and thereby produce descendants.

Cranach does not choose a different narrative of this story, but he keeps the representation of violence to the fires, storms, and destruction in the background. Painted doom as a substitute. And yet, Cranach's painting looks so modern and expressive, a little like something from a cartoon, that the painters of the "New Leipzig School" borrow from it even today.

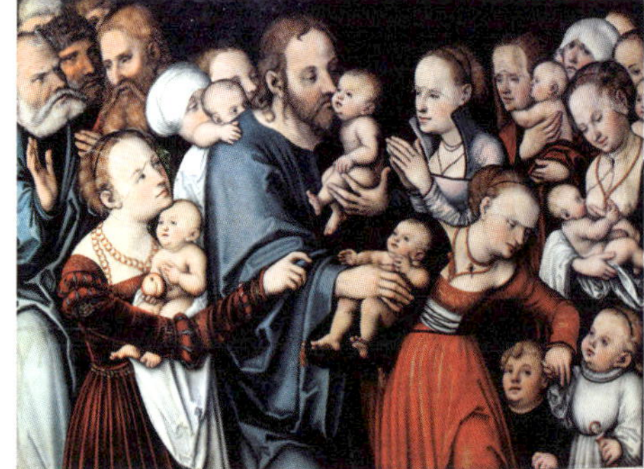

Christ Blessing the Children ca. 1538
Mixed media on beech wood
83.8 × 121.5 cm
Städelsches Kunstinstitut und
Städtische Galerie, Frankfurt am Main

In the years after the fall of the Berlin wall, there was a marked increase in art thefts from churches, museums, and galleries in the new regions of the Federal Republic. In 1992, eight paintings were stolen from Berlin's Stadtschloss, including the famous *Portrait of Luther as Junker Jörg*. At the time the value of all eight paintings came to almost 40 million dollars. The four perpetrators were later caught, and the paintings, damaged in the theft, were returned to the museum the same year. The men were found guilty of receiving stolen goods, but there was insufficient evidence to prove their involvement in the theft itself. In the 1990s, the clear-up rate for art theft was a quarter of all cases.

Cranach paintings were a popular form of booty. In 2009, the painting *Christ Blessing the Children* was stolen from a church in Norway, its material value at that point estimated at nearly 3 million dollars. Three days later the painting, also damaged, was found in a delivery van. Incidentally, Cranach painted many variations of this theme, of which some twenty copies have been preserved. In this children's blessing from the Städel Museum in Frankfurt, in a very cramped space, fifteen adults stand around Jesus, along with nine babies and children. A girl holds what appears to be a painted wooden doll.

In 1980, two altar wings were torn from their hinges, also from a church, this time near Wittenberg. The only clue that investigators could find to the

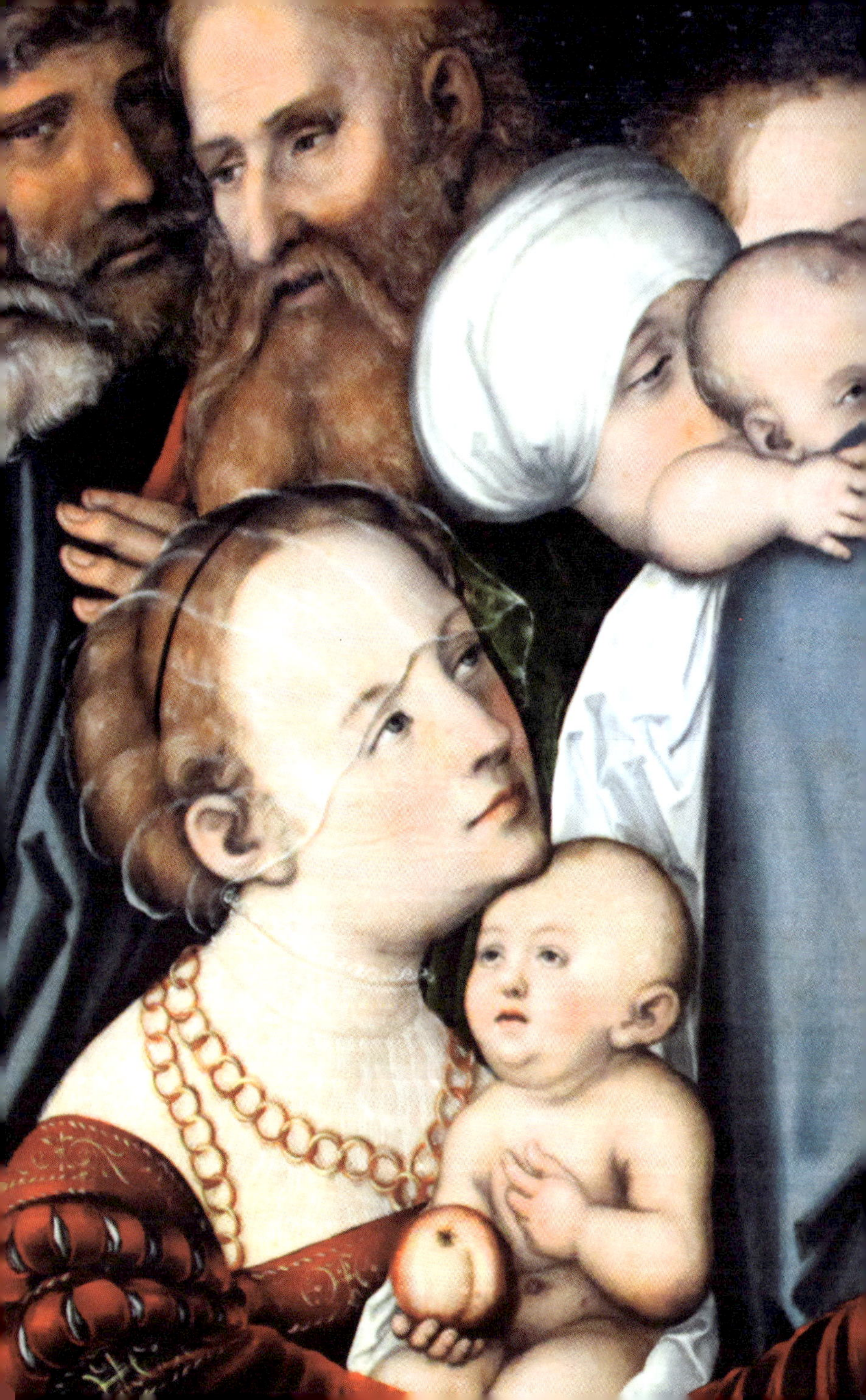

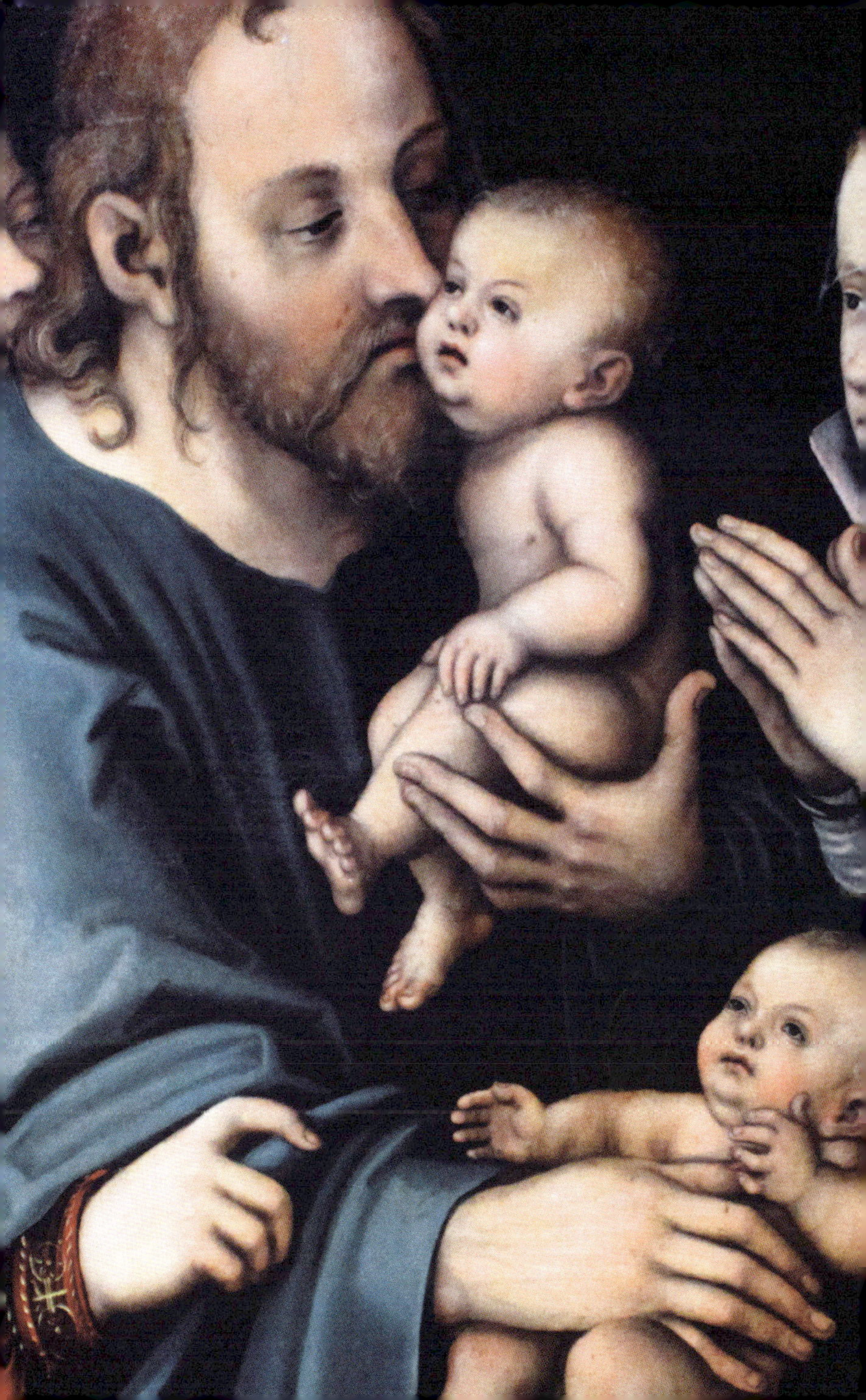

identity of the thief was the print of a trainer on the altar-cover: an East German brand, size 9. The perpetrators were never found, but the two altar wings with representations of Mary made by Cranach's workshop were found by chance twenty-seven years later. An antiques dealer in Bamberg bought them at auction and displayed them in his shop windows: the previous owner had converted the two altar wings into a kind of bar counter. In 2009, the work was valued at nearly 1.5 million dollars, and restoration must have cost just as much. The theft is already outside the statute of limitations and is no longer being investigated. The thieves are plainly being treated like the innocent children of Matthew 19:14—"Let the little children come to Me, and do not forbid them; for of such is the kingdom of heaven."

v → Venus

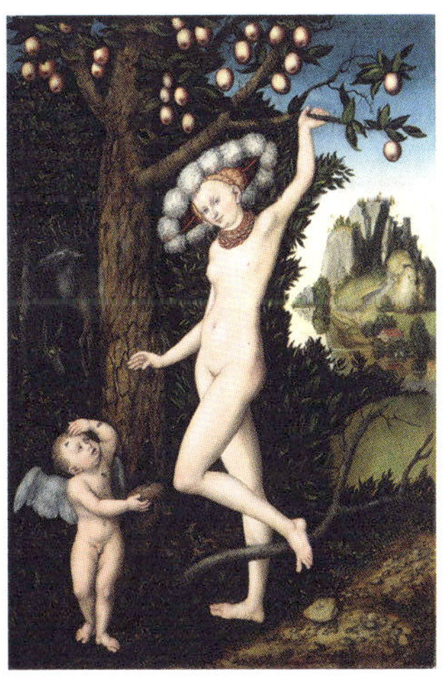

Cupid complaining to Venus 1526–27
Oil on wood, transferred to masonite
81.3 × 54.6 cm
National Gallery, London

It was at this time that naked people became
for the first time a subject of painting north
of the Alps. Sometimes the depictions are
life-size, sometimes only painted on small
panels that could be brought out as required.

Cranach painted many nudes for private
clients: alongside the biblical figures of Adam
and Eve, and Lot and his daughters, there
are the mythological women figures of Venus,
Caritas, Lucretia, or the sleeping nymphs of
the spring. He stages the newly awakened
interest in nature and the natural sensibilities
of Renaissance man.

The naked body is often covered by delicate,
almost invisible veils, which emphasize the
smooth skin even more than they conceal it.
A branch happens to grow in precisely such
a place that it covers the genitals. There is
play between showing and hiding, the indirect
thematization of sexuality under cover of an
exhortation to modesty. *Cupid complaining to
Venus*, painted in multiple variations, is a
fine example of the tense interplay between
desire and prohibition. Venus wears nothing
but a hat and jewelry; balancing on one leg,
she holds on to the branch of an apple tree.
A stag and a donkey in the background observe
the events. Little Cupid wanted to eat too
much honey, so the bees attacked and stung
him.

Giving oneself entirely to sweetness harbors a danger that we who merely watch luckily escape.

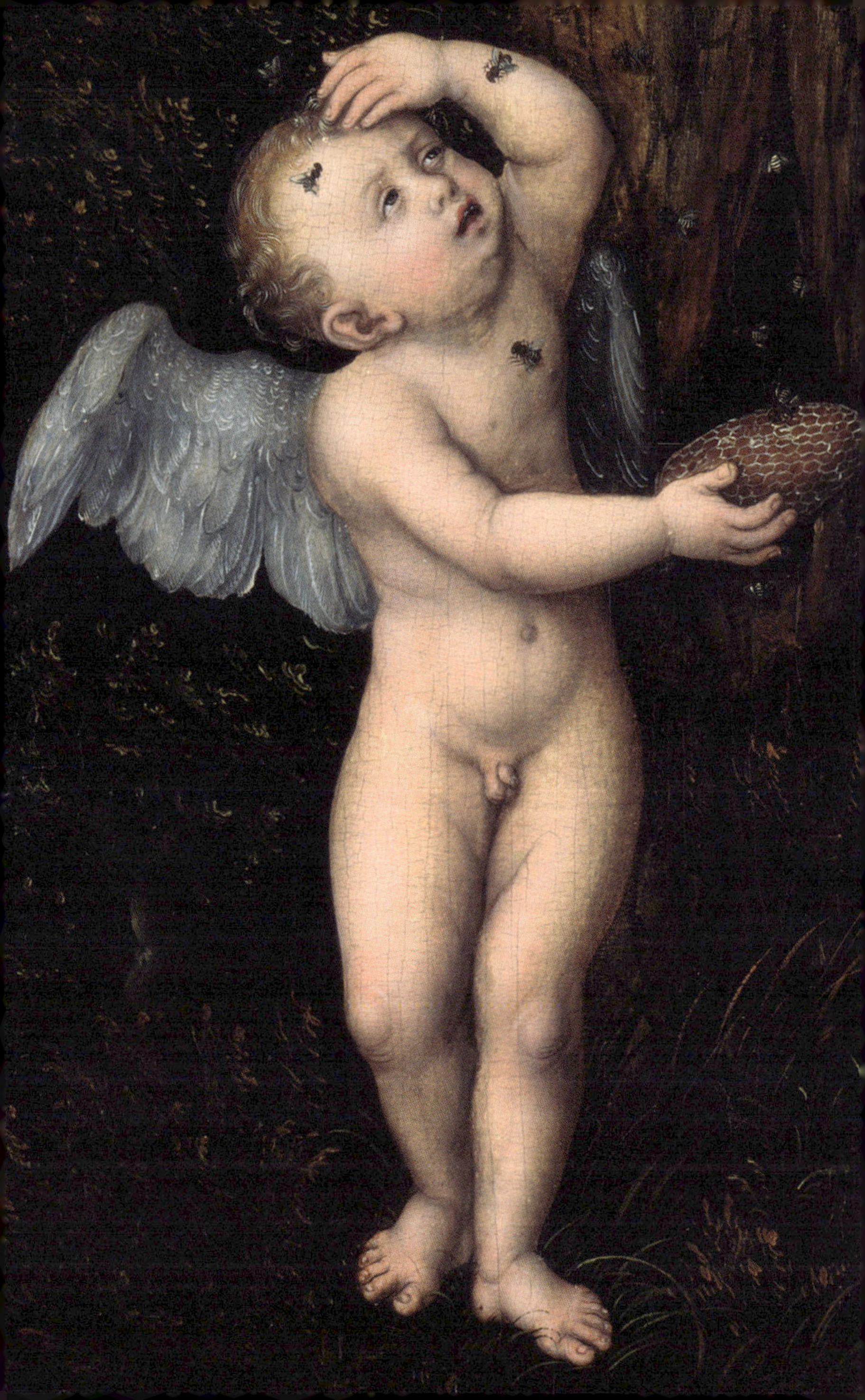

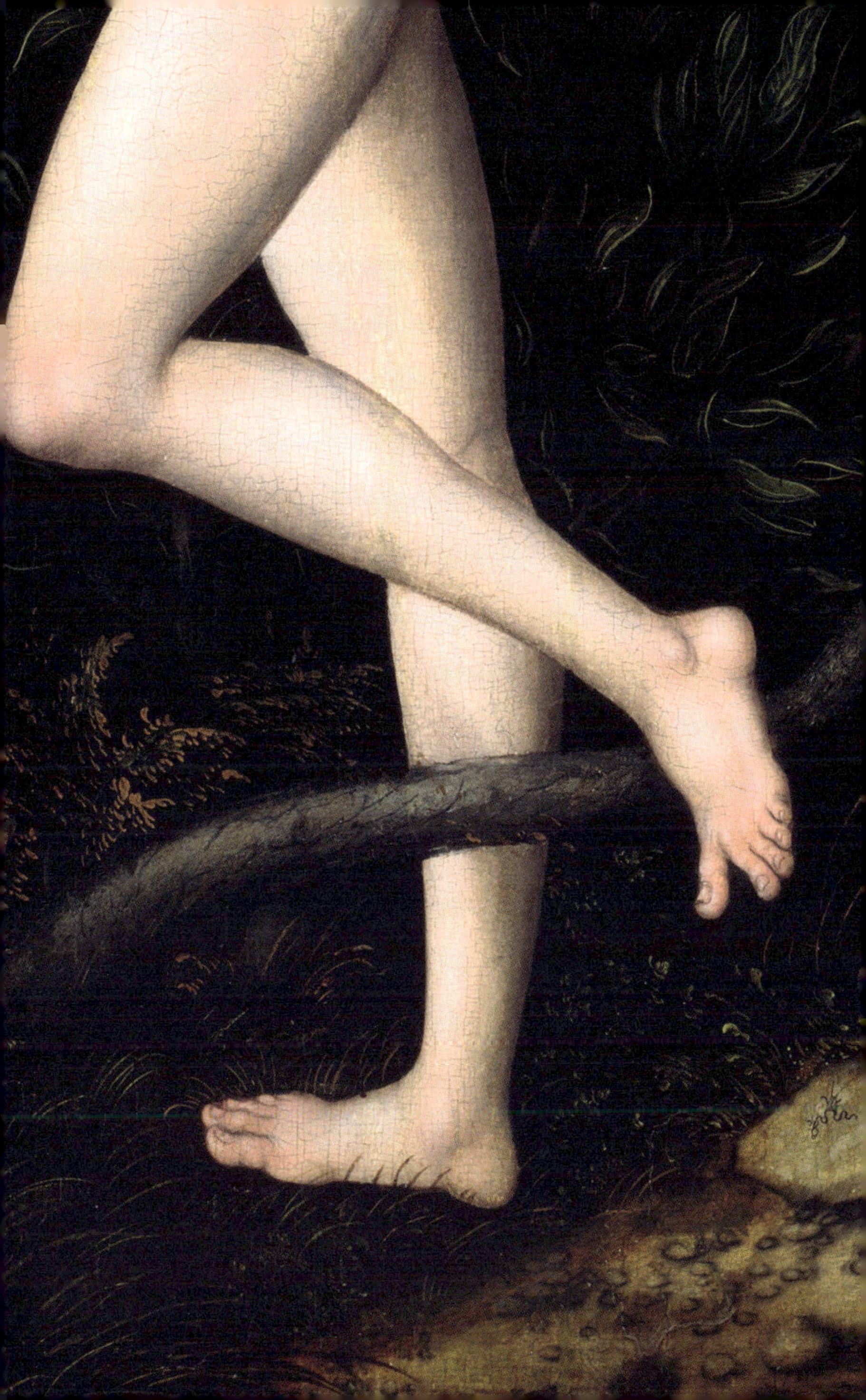

Cranach Court
1 Schlossstrasse in Wittenberg

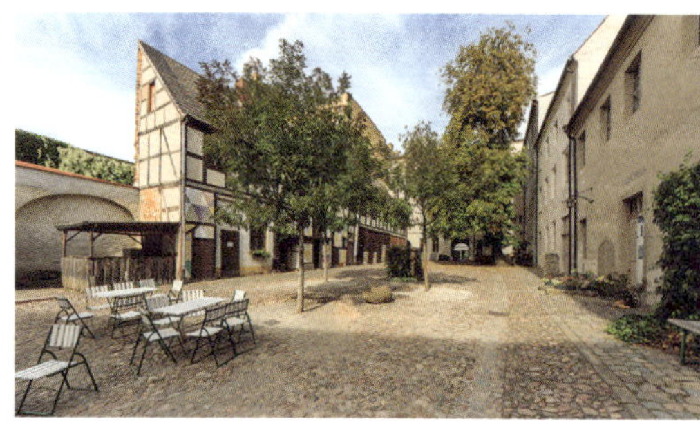

Lucas Cranach did not have a website, but if he lived today it would not be a surprise if he kept one to document and publicize his works. Because Cranach, as an artist in a time of transition from the Middle Ages to the modern period, was an early businessman and soon one of the wealthiest burghers in Wittenberg, who invested his fortune in property and rose to the position of councilor and mayor in his political career. Apart from an apothecary shop, a wine shop, and a printworks he ran a flourishing workshop in the court on Schlossstrasse, where he also trained apprentices. Along with the house at 4 Markt, 1 Schlossstrasse forms the "Cranach courtyards," where the print-room and exhibitions can be visited. Cranach sold his paintings not only to clients in the church and the nobility, but also to the burghers. He reproduced his drawings in the form of woodcuts and printed graphics. Lucas Cranach the Younger, who took over the business from his father, never worked as a court painter himself, but only ever as a freelance entrepreneur.

The fact that Cranach, just 450 years after his death, does now have an extensive website, the *Cranach Digital Archive* with the web address lucascranach.org, is thanks to an initiative by the Kunstpalast Museum Foundation in Düsseldorf and Cologne Technical University. Since 2009, a team, led by the art historian Gunnar Heydenreich in cooperation with numerous museums, research institutions, and churches

has been working to digitally index the work.
Over 2000 works are now accessible here: titled,
dated, and described.

If one studied a single Cranach painting from
this archive every day, it would take five and
a half years, not counting documents such as
receipts and shopping lists. In total, in the
eighty years of the Cranach workshop, from
father to son, 5000 works were produced.

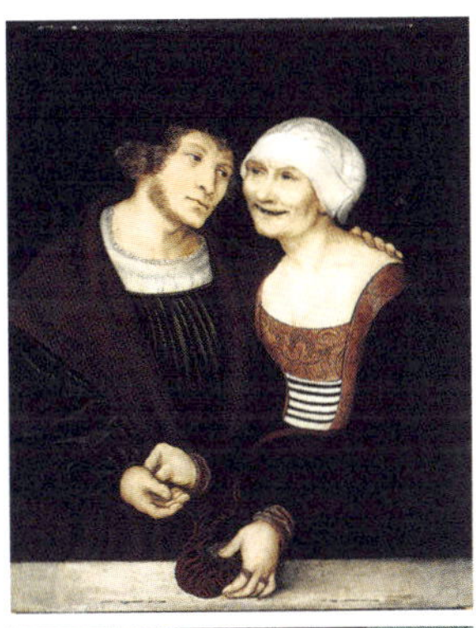

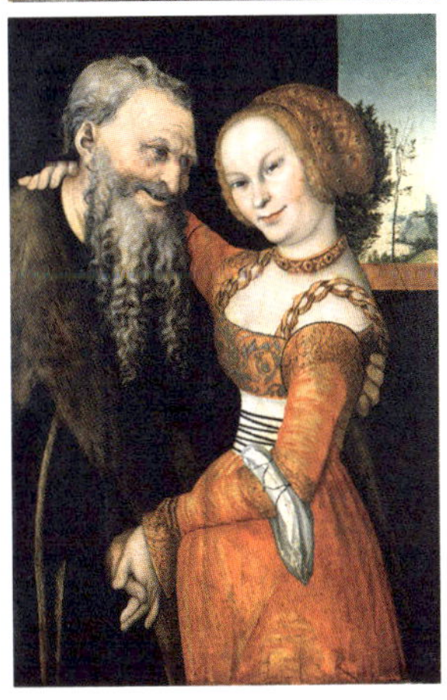

The Ill-matched Couple:
Old Woman and Young Man
ca. 1520–1522
Mixed media on beech wood
37 × 30.5 cm
Szépművészeti Múzeum, Budapest

The Ill-matched Couple ca. 1530
Oil on lime wood 86.7 × 58.5 cm
Germanisches Nationalmuseum,
Nuremberg

Shall we x-ray Cranach? Those invisible rays, with which one can illuminate the body and suddenly make bones and cell tissue visible, can also be used to investigate paintings: hidden layers come to light, along with rejections and over-paintings.

X-rays and infra-red photography penetrate to the layers below, all the way to the picture support, usually a stretched canvas or a wooden panel. Any errors in the wood are smoothed with oakum, a filler material made of silk fibers or flax. The pores of the support are closed by applying a white or grey ground. The under-drawing is applied to this chalk ground, analysis of which helps us today to distinguish father from son: Lucas Cranach the Elder drew continuous lines with brush and ink, while Lucas Cranach the Younger used short strokes in drawing chalk.

Investigation of the painting shows that the background color and the base of the flesh tones ("carnation") were applied next. The skin color tends, in line with the usual representational forms of the day, to be lighter for women and ochre or brownish for men. Color details can even be found in the preparatory drawing, which suggests further execution of the work by assistants.

The Cranachs painted with great economical intelligence: a volume is often produced from only two contrasting colors. The last delicate lines were set on the surfaces with the finest brushes before the glaze was applied.

The colors have changed in the course of time, and the skin is now covered with little cracks—the *craquelé*—both that of young women with old men and that of old women with young men, as revealed by the many variations of the popular theme of *The Ill-matched Couple*. With careful cosmetic facial treatment, the yellowed varnish is removed and Cranach's bright, gleaming colors exposed once more.

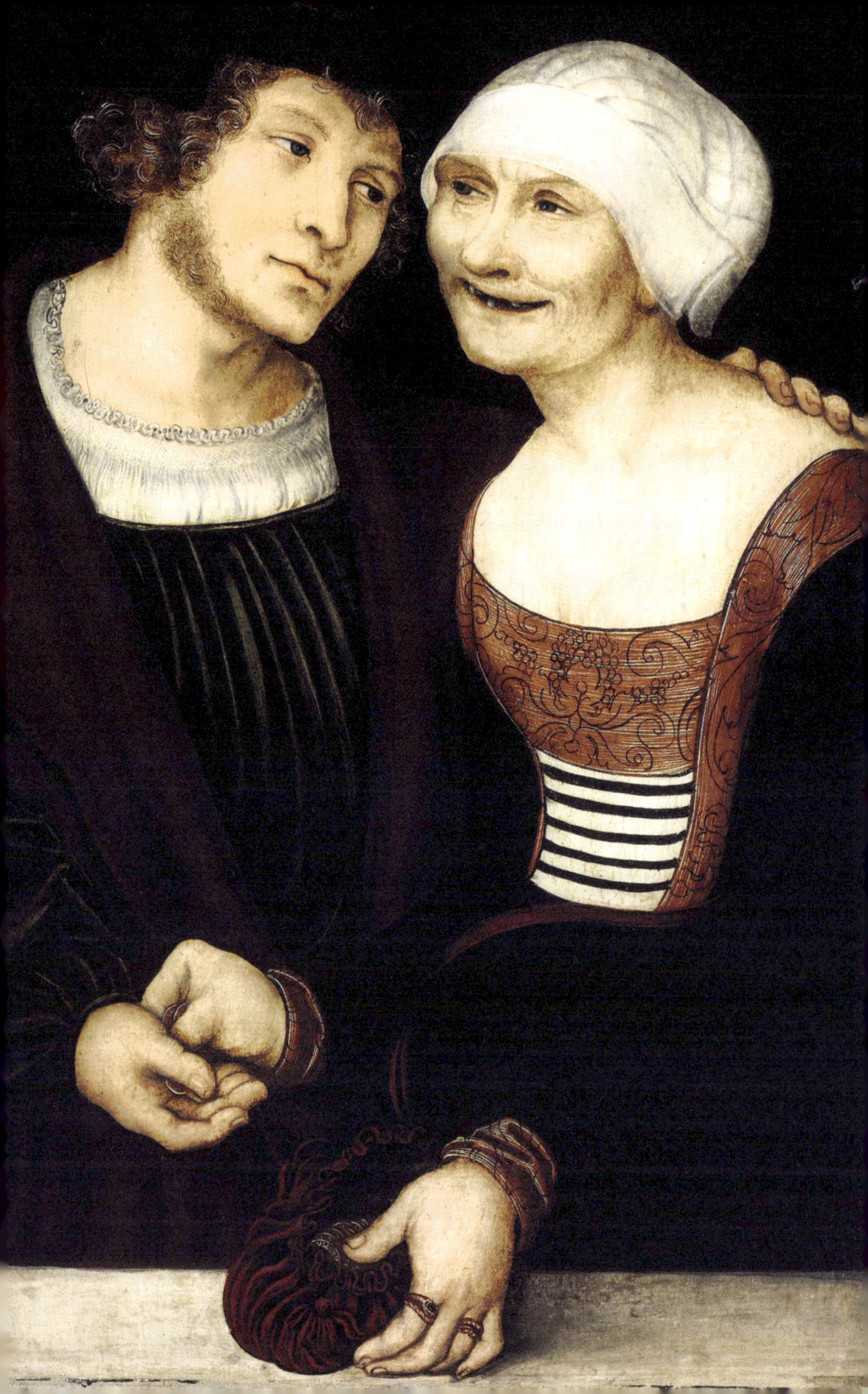

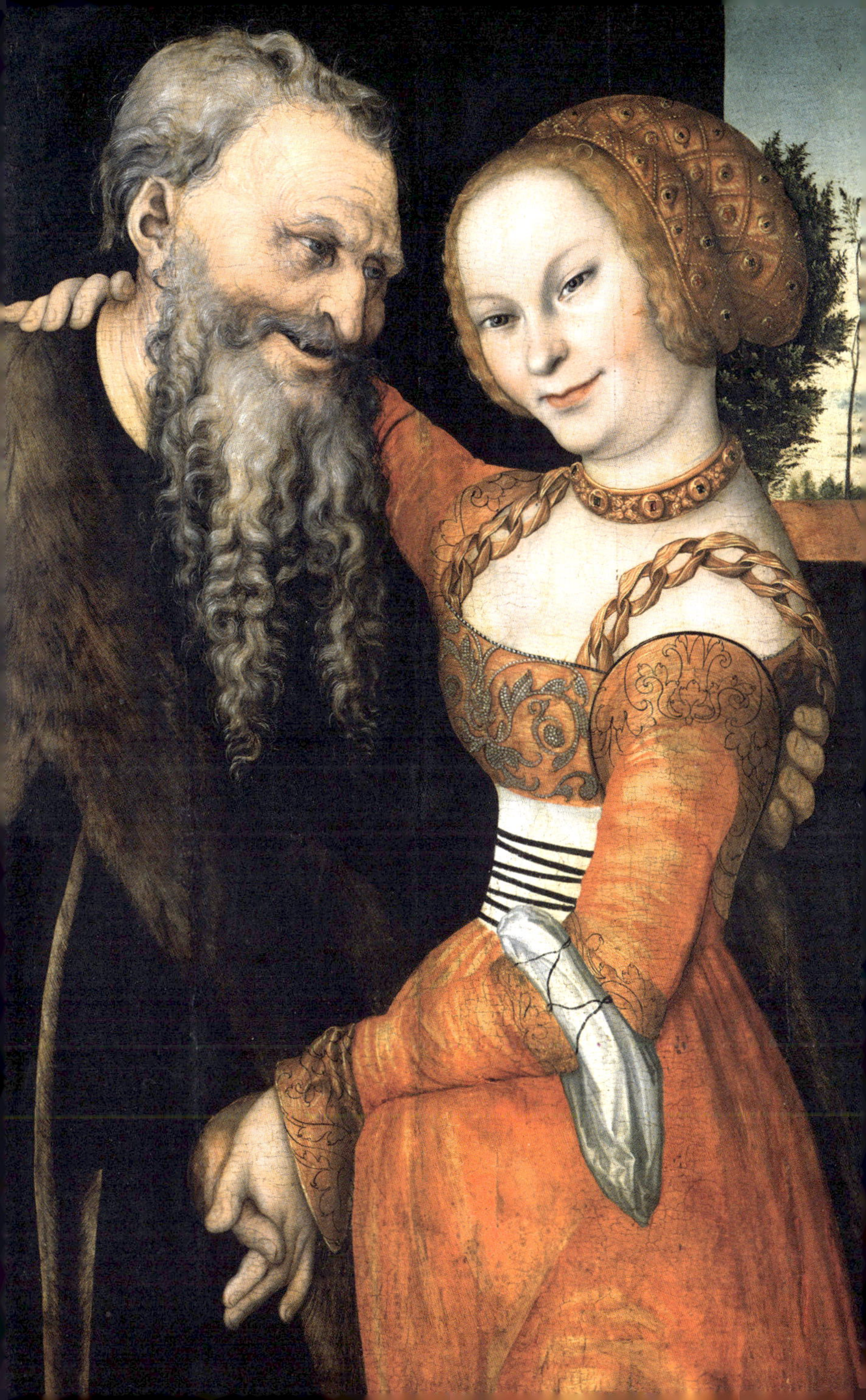

z → **Zooming in**

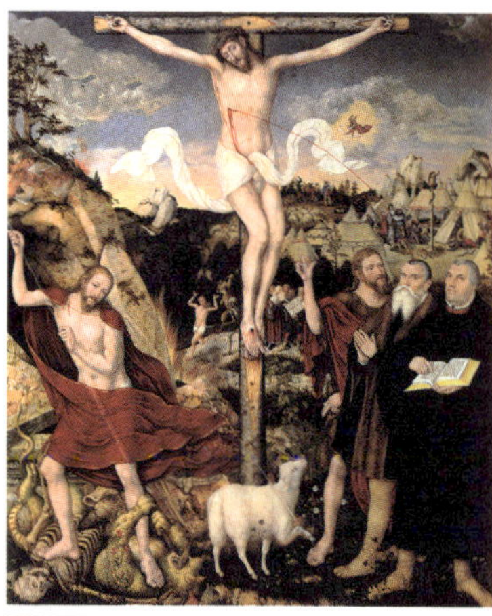

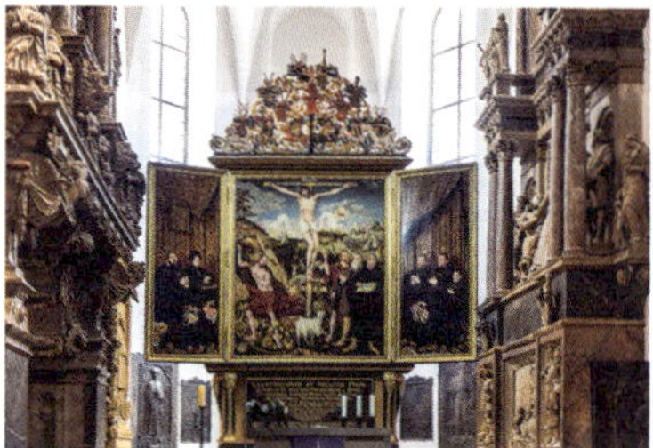

Lucas Cranach the Younger
Epitaph for John Frederick of Saxony
Altar reredos of the church of
St. Peter and Paul in Weimar 1555

If one wanted to write only about hands in Cranach, the gestures, the prophetic pointing figures, it would yield a whole book! The hands pray, they point, they guide our eyes to the detail of events—they invite us to zoom in.

Jesus's hands are nailed to the cross. A stream of blood from his wound hits Cranach the Elder, who is standing here between Martin Luther and John the Baptist. John the Baptist points at Jesus with the index finger of his right hand and with three fingers of his left at the soft, woolly, almost luminously bright Lamb of God. We wouldn't have missed it anyway! Luther holds the Bible and points to the text with a finger: the Word is all that counts. Cranach the Elder's hands are folded in prayer—even a painter sometimes has to set down his brush.

In the background a poor wretch runs away, hands upstretched, from Death and the Devil, while only a little way off Moses holds the Tablets of the Law, and another man points to them. An angel flies in the sky above, holding a scroll in his hands. The donors of the altarpiece, John Frederick the Magnanimous, his wife Sibylle von Cleve, and their three sons, sit lined up in a row praying on the side wings of the altar: black-robed figures against richly ornamented gold brocade curtains, all of them with their hands folded.

It is a work by Lucas Cranach the Younger, whose father had already died by the time it was completed. His father, the painter, looks at us from the picture, almost as if he is alive, a greeting that has outlasted the centuries.

Should we too fold our hands when we stand in front of these great paintings? In front of the Eves, the Martins, the Fredericks, the Emilias? My hands are not folded in prayer, but I rub my eyes with them when I stand in front of Cranach: because I can't believe what I'm seeing.

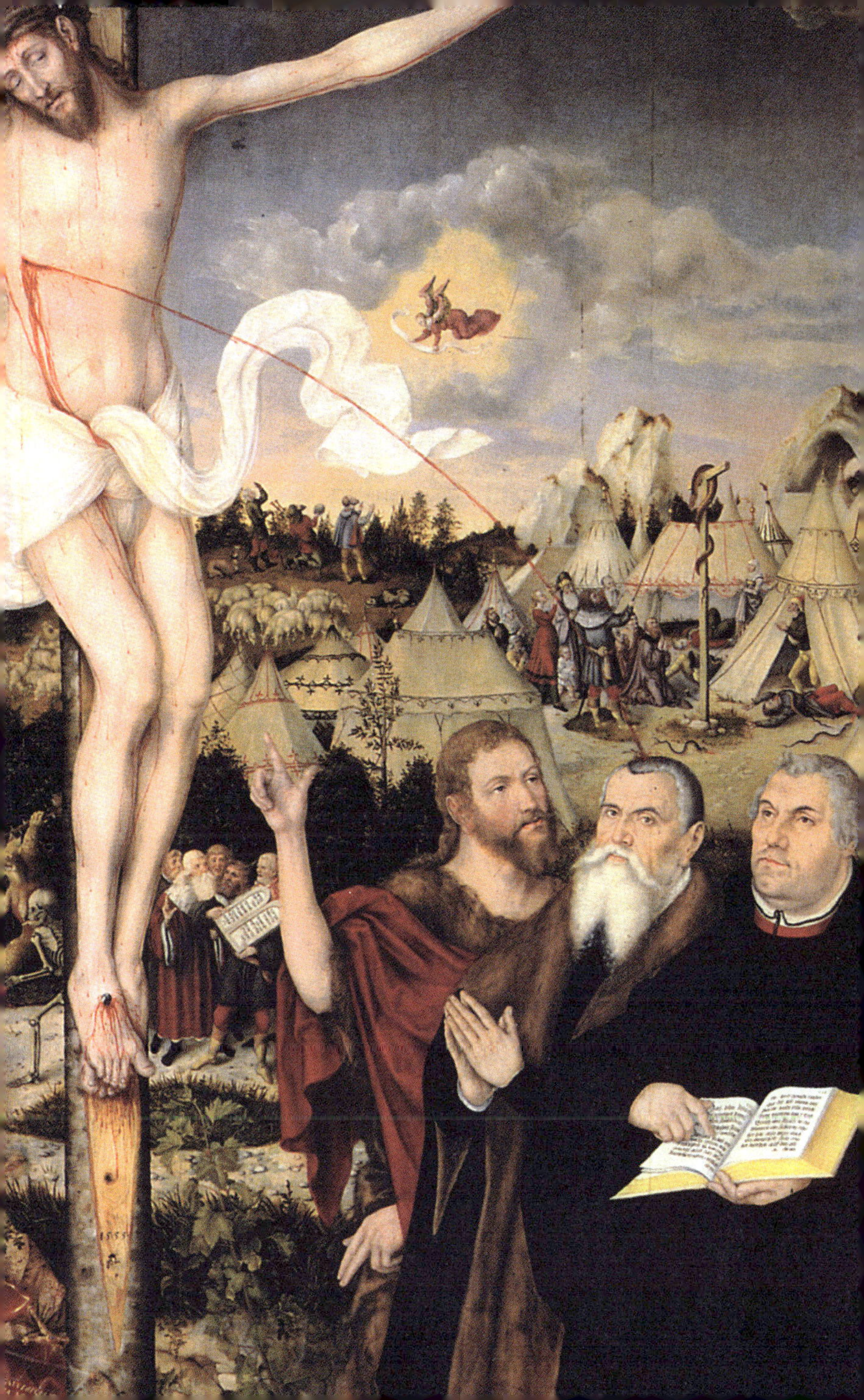

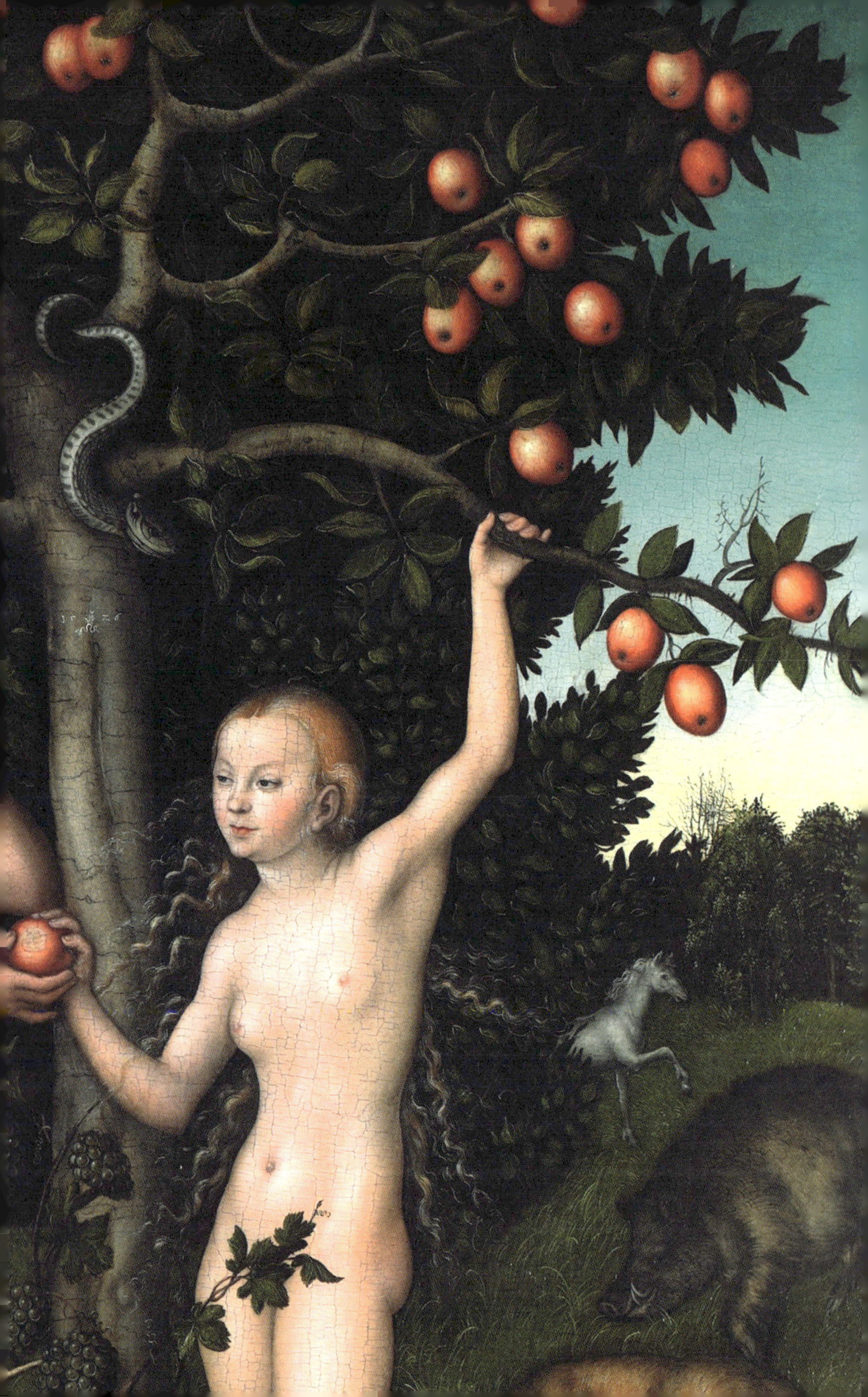

Colophon

The concept of the A–Z series is based
on an idea by Ulf Küster.

Copy editing   Hannah Young
Picture editing   Gabriela Wachter
Translations   Shaun Whiteside
Graphic design   Torsten Köchlin, Joana Katte,
   Theresa Peter
Typeface   Scto Grotesk A
Production   Thomas Lemaître
Reproductions   DLG, Paris
Paper   Munken Lynx, 150 g/m²
Printing   DZS GRAFIK, d. o. o., Ljubljana

© 2022 Hatje Cantz Verlag, Berlin, and author
© 2022 for the reproduced works:
   see photo credits

This publication was supported by:

KUNST
HISTORISCHES
MUSEUM
WIEN

Published by
Hatje Cantz Verlag GmbH
Mommsenstraße 27
10629 Berlin
www.hatjecantz.com

A Ganske Publishing Group Company

ISBN 978-3-7757-5180-3 (English edition)
ISBN 978-3-7757-5179-7 (German edition)

Printed in Slovenia

Cover illustration
Detail from
*The Princesses Sibylla (1515–1592),
Emilia (1516–1591) and Sidonia of Saxony
(1518–1575)* ca. 1535 (see pp. 34/35)

Frontispice
Detail from
Lucas Cranach the Elder
Self Portrait 1531
Mixed media on beech wood 45.2 × 35.5 cm
Stolzenfels Castle, Koblenz